a Brown Paper School book

THE NIGHT SKY BOOK

An Everyday Guide to Every Night

by Jamie Jobb

illustrated by Linda Bennett

Little, Brown and Company

Boston   Toronto   London

This Brown Paper School book was edited and prepared for publication at The Yolla Bolly Press, Covelo, California, between November 1976 and May 1977. The series is under the supervision of James and Carolyn Robertson. Production staff members are: Jay Stewart, Gene Floyd, Sharon Miley, and Joyca Cunnan.

Published simultaneously in Canada by
Little, Brown & Company (Canada) Limited.
Printed in the United States of America. T 10/77

HC: 10 9 8 7
PB: 20 19 18 17 16 15 14

BB

Library of Congress Cataloging in Publication Data

Jobb, Jamie.
    The night sky book.

    (A brown paper school book)
    1. Astronomy—Observers' manuals—Juvenile literature. I. Bennett, Linda. II. Title
QB164.J63   523.8'903   77-24602
ISBN 0-316-46551-8
ISBN 0-316-46552-6 pbk.

Long ago, many Indians believed
stars were really eyes in the night sky.
Some people still believe
stars watch over all of us at night.
This book is dedicated to these people.

The Night Sky

Turn on a light. Go to a movie. Watch TV. At night all kinds of lights go on when the sun goes down. Lights on signs blinking neon. Lights on posts. Lights on cars. Lights on the corner winking red, yellow, green. All these lights add up to one big blanket of light that chases away the night.

When you start any journey at night, you'll see glowing lights surrounding your hometown. Under this comfortable bright blanket, modern people lose sight of the most important light of all. Starlight. Starlight is everywhere, the one thing you'll see when you look anywhere into space.

Many people know stars and planets by name. You can too. To help you become familiar with the night sky, this book is divided into five parts. Part One tells how people find directions using the stars, even when they're lost at sea. Part Two shows how to find your place on earth or any other globe. Part Three tells about the zodiac, the moon, and time. Part Four sizes up the solar system. And Part Five looks at stars and other sights in the night sky. Clocks, sticks, rocks, record players, and other everyday objects can show you a lot about the stars. But the best way to learn about the stars is to watch them. Turn out the lights and go outside.

Thanks to

This book wouldn't be the same without these special people whom I'd like to thank. Doug McCoy for research and preparation of the Find That Constellation Games and Maps; Keith Muscutt for his interest in the ancients and their knowledge of the skies; Lynn Ferar for her care and concern for the language of the book. Also I appreciate suggestions along the way from Carlos Mundt, Eugene Schiavone, Linda Allison, David Katz, Robert Kourik, Peder Jones, Marilyn Burns, Helen Weinstein, George Robert Shipman III, Arthur Crummer, Gerald Pfeiffer, Patrice and Christine Manget, Marilyn Wylder, my sons, and all the other stars on earth.

Acknowledgments

The National Aeronautics and Space Administration provided the astonishing photographs of Mercury, Venus, earth, moon, Mars, Deimos, Phobos, and Jupiter. Also thanks to the Lowell Observatory for the photo of Pluto. The Yerkes Observatory of the University of Chicago provided the photos of the Great Nebula in Orion, the Pleiades, and the Andromeda spiral. Thanks to the Hale Observatories for the photo of the globular cluster of stars in Hercules.

Table of Contents

1

North and Night

The Stars and the Ancients

Before the invention of electricity, the eyes and minds of ancient people could easily wander through the night sky. Stars were familiar sights. Many people — especially explorers, sailors, and travelers — saw them as signposts in the sky. Travel was long and hard, but when anyone went anywhere, the stars were something they could count on. A traveler learned to follow certain bright stars as the stars moved night after night across the sky.

People knew the sky according to the groups of stars we now know as constellations. They knew the brightest stars by name and by their place within these constellations. People also understood the true nature of the zodiac.

They saw it as a big band of constellations circling the heavens. To them, the zodiac was a sacred pathway for the sun and planets to travel.

Ancient people told time by the sky. The sun and certain stars showed them the correct time of day or night. The moon told the time of the month. The stars measured the year and its seasons.

Planting, harvesting, festivals, and rituals were planned around the motions of the moon, planets, and stars. Because they did not live in bright cities or watch TV, the ancients knew the night sky very well. Over the centuries their knowledge of the sky added up. They passed it on to us.

Getting to Know the Sky at Night

Sure it sounds nice to say that stars pointed the way for early explorers. And it's easy to say that navigators found their way by the stars. But when you get right down to looking at the sky at night, it all seems very confusing.

How can you begin to know the night sky? First realize these important facts:

There is one star that will help you find all the others.

The movement of stars is very regular — night after night and year after year.

People all across the earth understand this movement, and some will be willing to explain it to you.

Explorers and navigators who used the night sky as a map knew the stars from experience and direct observation. They watched it night after night.

At Least Two Ways to Look at It

If you live in the country or a very small town, you'll see more stars than people who live in cities. But city people can see most of the major constellations and brightest stars during most of the month. In a city it's sometimes easier to spot constellations, because the sky isn't full of small stars to confuse things.

The best way to get to know the stars is to go camping for a few nights during different seasons of the year. You can camp on a roof, porch, or in a backyard. Or you can camp in a national park, wilderness area, or national forest. As long as the nights are clear, you'll see stars. Keep up with the weather reports.

Here are some things you should take: pen and pencils, your own journal or notebook, star maps that are easy to read, this book and others that help you, and a small penlight.

Camp Sights

Pitch your sleeping bag in a good spot before the sun goes down. Lie back and get relaxed with your head toward the north and your feet to the south. You know your directions, don't you?

By the time the sun sinks below the western horizon, you should be ready. Have a paper and pencil handy so you can take notes, if you are the kind of person who takes notes. Or if you are the kind who just likes to watch, then just watch. As the day dims, watch which stars come out first. Are you sure they're all stars? Some might be planets! A few might be something else, like a satellite or an airplane.

How can you tell the stars from everything else? Here are two hints: Because they're farther away, stars seem to move slower than anything else in the sky. Stars twinkle and blink and dance, unless they're directly overhead. Planets shine with a steadier light.

On-Your-Back World View

How you stand and sit has a lot to do with how you see. People can judge size and distance in front of them better than they can judge size and distance above their heads. Objects around you give clues as to how near or far away things are. But you don't have those kinds of clues in the night sky, especially when the moon, planets, and stars are right above you.

To really appreciate the stars, you need to see them on your back. This way you will be better able to judge their size and apparent magnitude. All objects in the night sky seem bigger, sharper, and clearer if you look at them while you're flat on your back. Your neck won't hurt so much either. Lie down and see.

The next time there is a full moon overhead, try this. Look up at the moon and get a good idea of how big you think it looks. Then measure with your arm extended full length. Count the number of fingers it takes to cover the moon.

Now lie down on your back and look straight up at the moon. Does it seem bigger or smaller? Measure again with your fingers to see for sure. What changed? The moon or you?

What's a Constellation?

The night sky hasn't changed a whole lot during the several thousand years that people have been gazing into it. People from every culture in every age have grouped the same stars into constellations, or outlines of stars that suggest something to whoever sees them.

Different cultures have given each star different names. Some stars have been grouped into different constellations, each with a different name too. There was much confusion for many years, until the 1920s when boundaries and the names of constellations were fixed by the International Astronomical Union.

Why are these stars grouped together at all? Minds try to fit things into patterns, especially things like points of light, such as far-off stars. Seeing constellations is like a follow-the-dots puzzle.

Many of the pictures people "drew" in the sky were based on stories about their gods, their mythology, their heavens.

Some of the pictures people imagined in constellations are easy to see.

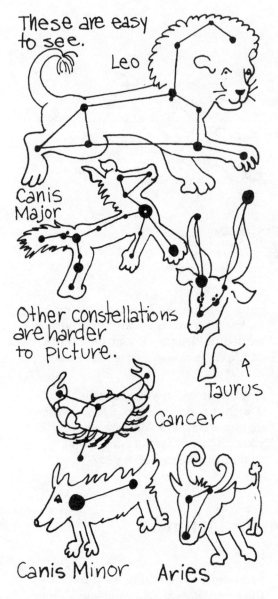

These are easy to see.

Leo

Canis Major

Other constellations are harder to picture.

Cancer

Taurus

Canis Minor   Aries

Star Movie Projector

Some people call this imaginary movie screen the "sky vault." Others call it "the celestial sphere." To picture what they're talking about, go get a grapefruit and eat it. Think about the movie screen as shaped like the inside of a completely eaten grapefruit — always curved and smooth. From any one spot on earth, you can see only half of the celestial sphere. The other half of the grapefruit is always below your horizon. Put the two halves of the empty grapefruit back together and that's the whole celestial sphere.

Constellation Names

Do you picture anything in these stars? For centuries people have put these stars into the same constellation. But they've seen it as different shapes. The Aztecs called it Cipactli (whale). In India it was known as Makaram (antelope). In Assyria it was called Munaxa (goat-fish). The Greeks thought it was "the gate of the gods." Certainly there are many ways to see the same stars.

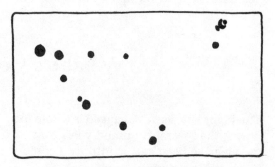

Imagine a movie screen high above the earth — somewhere between you and any group of stars. Light from the stars is projected onto the screen from behind. It's easy for your eyes to see this slow movie by starlight. And it's easy for your mind to connect stars with lines and to fill in the blanks to make a complete picture. Take some time and try it with any stars you see tonight.

This faint constellation belongs to the zodiac, along with Leo, Sagittarius, Aquarius, and all the rest. In most parts of the United States it can be seen on darker nights from August to December. Do you know what it's called?

Hint: It can be found between Sagittarius and Aquarius.   Answer: Capricornus

16

How to Play

"Find That Constellation"

This is a fill-in-the-dots game. It's a lot like the game people have played in the sky for centuries.

Look at the stars in the circle. Do you see the constellation? If you do, draw lines to connect the stars. If you want to, draw a picture of the creature that the constellation is named for. Write the name of the constellation under the circle. If you're not sure you've found it, use a pencil.

Around the edge of the circle are names and directions of nearby constellations. They are found in the same part of the night sky, next to the mystery constellation. If you need help, use star maps in this book and others.

Other hints are given under the circle. These include when and where to see the constellation in the sky. The answer can be found on the page listed at the bottom of the game.

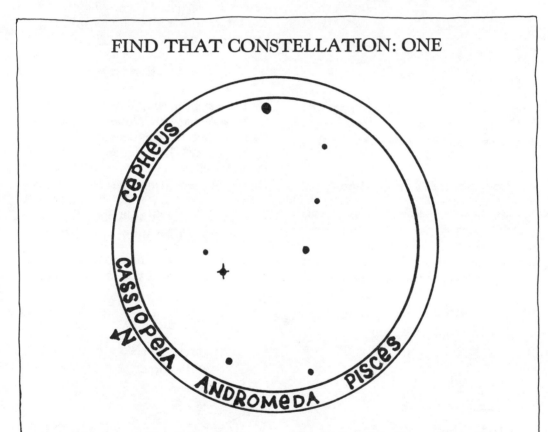

FIND THAT CONSTELLATION: ONE

Part of this constellation makes a large "square." It is a major reference point for navigators. Two of these stars are very close to the line that marks the starting point for telling all time and for pinpointing locations in the sky and on the planet.

Hint: Horses in the sky must have wings.

When to look for it: Begins rising in early September and remains one of the major fall constellations. It is seen all over North America until late March.

Answer on page 23.

Tin Can Planetarium

You can use tin cans to make a simple star projector. Pick a constellation you know. Draw it on a piece of paper. Make sure it's the same scale as the can. Put the paper over the end of the can with the tin still attached. Use different-sized nails to show the different brightness of each star.

Use the paper to make a pattern.

When you're done, stick a flashlight into the open end of the can. Go to a dark room. Flick the flashlight switch, and presto!

Do-It-Yourself Constellations

One way to learn about constellations is to pick some stars and group them any way you want to. Give these constellations names you can remember, like the Grand Canary or the Royal Donut or whatever picture comes to mind. Use a pencil to draw the stars and connect the lines to make constellations. You may want to change these later. When you've got a constellation you like, you can draw it in pen and ink and put it into your own book of constellations.

It's fun to make your own constellations. But after a while you'll face the same problem everyone does about naming your own constellations — no one else will know what you're talking about. At some point you'll need to learn the names and shapes of constellations as the International Astronomical Union outlined them.

Constellation Prize

By the way, Running Rat is known to most people as Ursa Major, the Big Bear. Can you find the Big Bear in the northern night sky? Look among the stars in this constellation. Can you find the Big Dipper in there somewhere?

"Running Rat in Space" or " My First Book of Stars"

You'll get to know the constellations sooner and better if you know how to

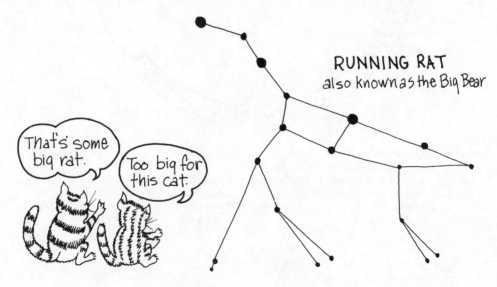

RUNNING RAT
also known as the Big Bear

That's some big rat.

Too big for this cat.

draw them and learn a few myths and stories about them. The best way to do this is to start a little journal to keep all the drawings and stories together. Stationery and art supply stores sell little blank books. The pages are completely blank so you can draw and write all over them. A small one costs a couple of dollars. Get one of these books and you can keep track of each new constellation you get to know.

It's a good idea to learn constellations one at a time. Watch one for several nights in a row. It will take a whole year for

you to see all the stars that will pass over your house. So take your time.

There are a few stories about special stars and constellations in this book. But there are always more star stories than any one book can tell. Most libraries have several books about star lore, Greek and Roman mythology, sailing myths, and other stories about stars. Ask a librarian if you need help. You will never stop finding stories about the stars. Your book can get fancier as you go along, especially as you learn the system for mapping stars.

FIND THAT CONSTELLATION: TWO

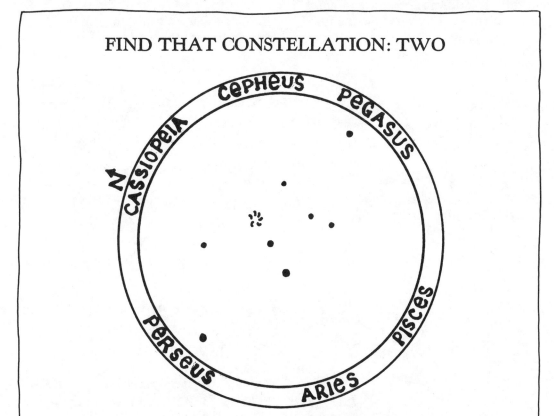

These stars mark the location of a special spiral object. It is so very distant that you can't see anything farther away from you. The light from it is over 2,000,000 years old.

Hint: She is the daughter of a King and Queen who spin around the North Star.

When to look for it: Begins rising in September and becomes a major fall constellation. It is seen everywhere in North America until May.

Answer on page 25.

Above All Else Know North

Are you good at directions or do you get lost easily? Most of the time people don't stop to think about directions. North is north, and south is wherever it is. Most people find directions the same way any good navigator does — they watch for landmarks, things that catch their eye. Of course, if you've never been to a place, then you need to know directions.

Do you know exactly where north is? Put this book down right now and point to true north. Can you do it without using a compass?

Shadow Stick Trick

Boy Scouts have a very wise way of finding directions without a compass. It's good to know this trick when you're outside feeling lost and lonesome. All you need is one sunny day and one straight stick, about a foot long. This is more accurate if you do it around noon. But it is close enough at other times of the day.

Hint: As you read this, the sun floats farther toward the west.

1. Put a straight stick into the ground, so it doesn't cast any shadows. The stick should point straight at the sun.

sun moves
west

2. Go rest for an hour at least. If you're lost, don't worry about being lost.

3. Come back when the shadow is about six inches long. The sun will have moved farther west.

4. Which direction does the shadow point? Can you figure it out?

S
90°

Polar Points and Paradoxes

North and south each suddenly stop at a certain spot on the earth. When anyone goes there, they know they can't go any farther in that direction. It's too cold anyway, so people don't go there very often.

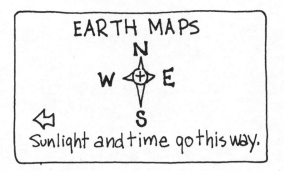

Where does north end?
Where does south end?
Where does east really end?
Where does west end?

The Difference Between Earth Maps and Sky Maps

Astronomers, explorers, and travelers wouldn't be able to move if they didn't know where to find north and all the other directions. To figure this out, they use maps and charts. But anyone who doesn't know the difference between earth maps and sky maps will still be lost. Unless the maps say otherwise, they are oriented this way:

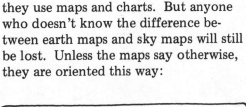

Looking down onto earth.

Looking up into the sky.

Land Under the Lodestar

The Norsemen were the Northmen. Maybe you know them as the Vikings. They were the ancient ancestors of people who now live in Norway, Denmark, Sweden, Iceland, and Greenland. The Vikings were fierce seamen who rode in dragon ships. They plundered much of northern Europe a thousand years ago, long before the Spanish, English, and other Europeans set out on the Atlantic in search of the Orient and the New World.

Many people now believe the Vikings were the first Europeans to see North America, although the Norsemen didn't establish a permanent settlement. In 982 A.D. Eric the Red discovered Greenland by following directions from other Vikings who had been blown off course. Eighteen years later, Eric's son, Leif, sailed west and discovered Baffin Island, Labrador, and Newfoundland. He may have ventured as far south as what is now Boston.

Viking ships were fast but they were not built to take storms. To get out of a storm's way, Viking ships often "ran before the wind." This caused them to venture many miles off course. But Vikings weren't lost for long. They had the lodestar to guide them after storms blew away and the night was clear. This is how they found Greenland, land under the lodestar. Lodestar almost always means the North Star.

The Viking Solar Stone

The Vikings had a simple navigation instrument that always helped them find north. It will help you understand why they have every right to be called Northmen. Historians call it the solar stone or the bearing dial. In the daytime it was used to indicate the sun's shadow at noon. At noon this shadow points north. For the Vikings, north was home.

The solar stone could also be used at any time of night to find north. The Vikings simply sighted the lodestar through the dial's shadow stick. It took a steady hand to use the instrument in rough seas. But after the Viking found north, he could determine the other directions by looking at the dial. Then he would set the pointer on the dial toward the direction he wanted to go.

A solar stone and how to use it

Lodestar

bearing dial

shadow stick

pointer stick

This arm points north.

Set pointer stick in the direction you are going.

Sight the lodestar with the shadow stick.

Turn the dial until north lines up with the sight line to the star.

Questions About the Solar Stone

Why will this instrument work in daytime only at noon?

Hint: Watch which way the sun's shadow points tomorrow morning after sunrise or tomorrow evening before sunset.

Remember the Boy Scout stick trick for finding north? Can you figure out a way to use the solar stone to tell directions the same way Scouts do with a stick?

This instrument works best in the far north. If you live in Miami, Key West, southern Texas, or any other subtropical place, this dial won't work as well in the summer. Why not?

Answer to Find That Constellation One: Pegasus (see map, page 30)

One Star That Does Not Move
(Very Much)

Many Indians who lived in North America centuries ago were nothing like the Vikings and other Europeans who later discovered North America. These Indians never saw the sea, nor did they travel upon it. They may have heard stories about the sea, but they didn't need to know how to navigate on the open ocean. They were land people.

These land people still had something in common with the Vikings and other sea people. They knew the four directions, the moon, the sun, and other stars. The Navajo were such a tribe. Around 500 years ago, they moved from somewhere "north" to the harsh and hot desert lands of what is now northern Arizona.

In the Navajo's myths of creation, it is clear that the Indians also knew the most helpful star in the universe. They called it "The Star That Does Not Move." This is the same lodestar of the Vikings — the star over the north pole, or Polaris, the North Star.

Navajo Creation Myth

This is a story from the Navajo myths of creation: First Woman, First Man, and Coyote the trickster had many trials and tribulations in the four lower worlds, so they moved on to the fifth world. All three of them were very dissatisfied with

the night sky in the fifth world. In fact the sky was very boring all day and all night. The sky had only the sun and moon. No stars. No planets. Nothing else.

First Man, First Woman, and Coyote decided to change it. Coyote scattered bright mica dust around the heavens, and the stars were born. Then he grouped the stars into constellations, so people could make pictures in the sky and give the stars names. First Woman helped

Coyote give the moon many faces, so it could change expressions all during the month.

Then at the pole position in the heavens, First Man placed The Star That Does Not Move. First Man knew that if people started with this star, they could know the whole night sky. To help everyone find this special star, First Man placed the seven stars of the Little Bear around it. The Star That Does Not Move was at the tail of the Little Bear.

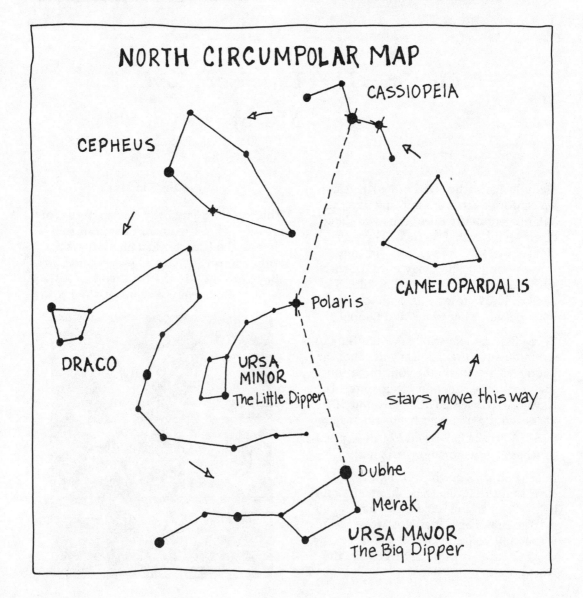

NORTH CIRCUMPOLAR MAP

CASSIOPEIA

CEPHEUS

CAMELOPARDALIS

Polaris

DRACO

URSA MINOR
The Little Dipper

stars move this way

Dubhe

Merak

URSA MAJOR
The Big Dipper

Vikings called it the lodestar. Navajo Indians called it the Star That Does Not Move. Chinese knew it as the Great Imperial Ruler of Heaven. Arabs called it Al Kiblah and the early Greeks named it Phoenice. Today people call it the North Star, Polaris, or the Pole Star. No matter what name is used, most people in the earth's Northern Hemisphere know it is the "most useful star in the heavens." You'll always find it in the same place — night after night, hour after hour. Although it seems motionless, the Pole Star does move in a very slight circle each night. Most people can't notice this movement, but machines can.

Get to know this star. It is a very special star for earth. There is no other object in the night sky like it. Every day of your life and everywhere you go, keep this little third-magnitude star fixed in the top of your mind. It will help you find north and all the other directions when you get lost. It will guide you home as it has countless other explorers across earth.

North Circumpolar Map

These stars and constellations revolve around the North Star. They can be seen on any cloudless night from anywhere in North America. They spin like a very slow record on a turntable.

Turn the book around and look at these stars many ways. Hold the map upside-down. It doesn't matter, because these constellations are never really upside-down. One round-the-pole constellation, Camelopardalis, is very hard to see with unaided eyes.

Answer to Find That Constellation Two: Andromeda (see map, page 30)

How to Find the North Star Every Night

Find north, using a compass to show the general direction. Or you can use a shadow stick or a solar stone in the daytime, and then remember where north is at night.

Then find the Big Dipper, the Little Dipper, and Cassiopeia — three of the brightest constellations in the North. Find Merak and Dubhe, the two bright stars in the Big Dipper. They are the two stars farthest from the Big Dipper's handle. They are the pointer brothers. They point to Polaris, the last star in the handle of the Little Dipper.

Platters That Matter or Why Polaris Doesn't Move (Very Much)

Would a Beatles' album, or anybody else's record for that matter, be worth one single note if there weren't a hole in the middle of it? Of course not. But what does this have to do with the stars?

Go to a record player and find out. Put on a record — some kind of good thinking music. But don't start the machine yet. Imagine that the record is the earth, and the North Pole is the spindle that the record hole fits onto. Now start the earth spinning.

Put another record onto the spindle, in position to fall when it is ready. Imagine this record is a movie screen showing the northern stars. If you were spinning on the turntable earth below, how would these stars seem to move? Look at the spindle and imagine Polaris where the hole in the top record is. Polaris does not seem to move as the earth spins around and around below it. Why?

There is no South Pole star, but there is a point in space above the South Pole. All the southern stars spin around this point.

FIND THAT CONSTELLATION: THREE

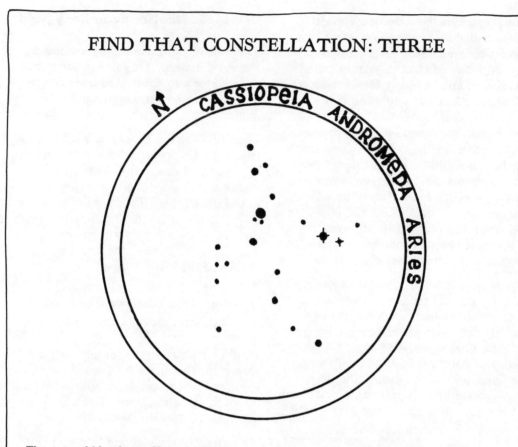

These stars hide a hero. He is chasing after a princess, but he's never able to reach her. The constellation is located in the Milky Way. It contains a famous slow-blinking star.

Hint: The hero was a son of Zeus.

When to look for it: In the far north, it can be seen every night. Elsewhere in North America, it rises in mid-October and can be seen high in the sky until late May.

Answer on page 29.

Sailing Along the Star-Path

The Pacific Ocean covers half the globe. It is so big that the peoples of Asia and Europe took several centuries to realize that the Pacific connects both East and West into one whole wide world.

But in the last 4,000 years a quiet people known as the Polynesians charted and inhabited one hundred scattered and small islands throughout this vast ocean. Many Europeans who later heard about Polynesian sailing feats weren't willing to believe that this was possible.

It does seem unbelievable. No compass, astrolabe, quadrant, or other navigation instrument guided the Polynesians. Only the sun and other stars led them across the ocean. They knew the right time of year and time of night to expect certain stars in certain places. They knew which star was important because it pointed to other stars and constellations. They called their way of navigation, "following the star-path."

Make Your Own Solar Stone

A solar stone does not necessarily need to be made of stone. Vikings used wood as well as stone to make these direction finders. You can use cardboard, wood, a flat round stone, or any other material that is easy for you to work with. If you want to make one, take your time and make a nice one.

The Polynesian Triangle

By the end of the 16th century, when the first Europeans saw the first Poly-nesians, the Polynesians had settled most of the islands in a gigantic triangle of ocean covering an area about as big as Africa. These islands, except for Ao-tearoa (New Zealand), were small dots in a big ocean. They were so small that people soon overpopulated them. There wasn't enough room for everyone, so some sailed out to find new islands along the star-path.

The Magic Calabash

Calabash is another word for a bottle gourd. Gourds are hard-shelled fruits from the same family of plants that produces watermelons, pumpkins, squash, and cucumbers. People have used bottle gourds for many things including dishes, ladles, and tobacco pipes.

Polynesian sailors had a unique way to use bottle gourds. They used a special

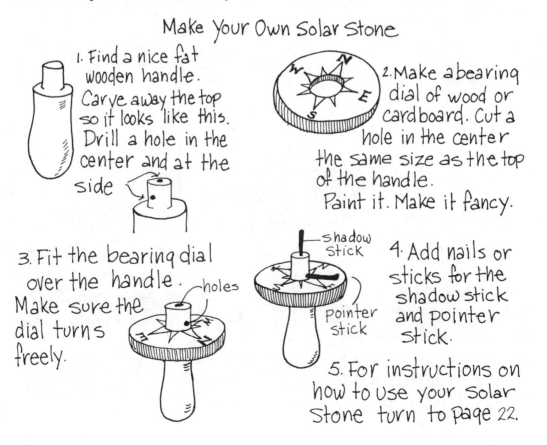

Make Your Own Solar Stone

1. Find a nice fat wooden handle. Carve away the top so it looks like this. Drill a hole in the center and at the side

2. Make a bearing dial of wood or cardboard. Cut a hole in the center the same size as the top of the handle. Paint it. Make it fancy.

3. Fit the bearing dial over the handle. Make sure the dial turns freely. —holes

shadow stick

pointer stick

4. Add nails or sticks for the shadow stick and pointer stick.

5. For instructions on how to use your solar stone turn to page 22.

calabash to help them sight the North Star, and they found Hawaii. That may sound a little far-fetched. In fact, some scientists believe this whole story is a myth. There was no such navigation instrument as the magic calabash they say. Do you believe it? Make one for yourself and see.

Make a Magic Calabash

You can make a magic calabash for your own home latitude. Find a gourd in the produce department of the supermarket. Fall is the best time to look. If you can't find one in the market, you can grow your own in a sunny summer spot.

If you grow gourds, let them dry in the sun after the plants die back in the fall. Be sure the shell is completely hard before you start to make the calabash. You can also use any other container besides a gourd as long as it holds water. But it won't be a real calabash!

How to Do It

Take a calabash and using a sharp knife, cut a level top — carefully! Then drill one hole so you are able to see the North

Make a Magic Calabash

Pick a calabash (or maybe two in case you goof).

Cut the top level.

This is the tricky part.
Polaris
Drill one hole. Keep the gourd level. Hold it in front of one eye. With the other eye, sight Polaris so it is just touching the far rim of the calabash. Mark the spot.

Polaris
20°
water   Horizon
This angle is your home latitude.

Drill four more holes around the rim of the gourd. Make them the same distance down the side of the gourd as the first hole.

Fill your calabash with water. If no water spills from the holes, it's level.

Star right on the rim of the calabash when you are holding it level.

Drill four more holes around the rim. These should be the very same distance down the side of the gourd from the top as the first one is.

Your home latitude is the angle between the water level and rim as shown in the illustration. In Hawaii, it is about 20 degrees N latitude. But if you live in the far north, all the holes will be very far from the rim. Why?

How to Use It

To accurately sight Polaris, it is very important to hold the calabash level with the horizon. To make sure of this, the Polynesians filled the gourd with water. They knew exactly when the gourd was not level, because water spilled out of any one of the five holes. This would be a big problem on nights with rough seas and storms.

How Hawaiians Used It

Before setting out, a priest who was to sail with the boat would make a calabash in Hawaii. For the magic to work, the priest performed a special ceremony with a strong gourd. Then he made the holes around the rim at 20 degrees north latitude. When the gourd was finished, they sailed south.

Months later the ship would return with the prevailing current, but this north-flowing current runs far to the east of

Hawaii. When the priest felt the boat getting close to the home islands, he would get out the calabash and sight Polaris. From then on, he would watch the North Star until the night when the star seemed to be just kissing the rim of the calabash. On that night, he would know it was time to leave the north-running current and head westward toward the home islands.

Polynesian Pointer Stars

To Polynesians, Polaris was important for finding Hawaii and other North Pacific islands. But when they traveled south of the equator where Polaris could not be seen, they relied on other stars.

According to the Polynesian system for steering by the stars, there are two kinds of stars more important than the North Star. First are stars that rise on the horizon at an expected time of night and season and point to other stars that follow on that same point.

The other kind are stars directly overhead that point down to an island. They are usually very bright. These stars change during the year, but the island people remember them all. What are the compass stars and zenith stars for your latitude? Put them in your star book.

Answer to Find That Constellation Three: Perseus (see map, page 30)

Polynesian Pointer Stars

Horizon
Compass Stars rise on the horizon.

Zenith stars are right overhead.

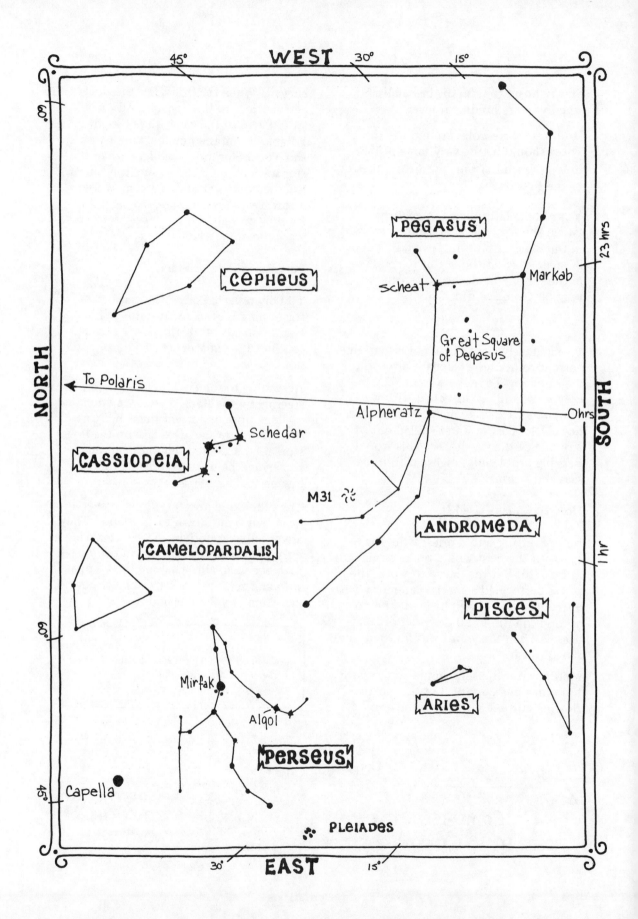

FIND THOSE CONSTELLATIONS: MAP ONE

This map contains all stars and shapes found in Find That Constellation games One, Two, and Three. You can see these stars in the fall sky. They will be directly overhead at these times: late October (10 p.m.), late November (8 p.m.), late December (6 p.m.).

Greek myths tell the story of Andromeda, daughter of Queen Cassiopeia and King Cepheus. Andromeda was a very good-looking princess, and her mother bragged about this a lot. This angered the gods, so Andromeda was chained to the rocks and left there for the monsters of the sea. Of course, any beautiful princess in danger needs to be rescued! In the myth the hero who rushed to save Andromeda was Perseus, son of Zeus. But in the sky it seems as if Andromeda is being carried to safety by Pegasus, a flying horse from a whole other story.

Pegasus is the Winged Horse. For navigators and skywatchers, the "Great Square of Pegasus" is a key corner of the sky. The line from Algenib through Alpheratz is very close to the line that marks the beginning point for mapping the whole sky. This is the "O hour angle." It helps all navigators find the direction and location of everything else in the sky and on earth. Alpheratz is the zenith star on midnight of the first day of fall. This means it is right overhead.

Andromeda is the Chained Princess. With Pegasus, she shares Alpheratz. This star is actually in two constellations! Andromeda helps people locate the farthest point you can ever see with your own two eyes — the Great Spiral Nebula, also known as M31. This beautiful star-island is 2,200,000 light years away. It is a galaxy, like our own Milky Way. Some night follow a line from Polaris through

Schedar in Cassiopeia. It points to the Great Spiral. The nebula is not very bright, so look for it on a dark night. You'll know it when you see it, because it's fuzzy and not a pinpoint like a star.

Perseus, the Hero, follows the other constellations by about two hours. If you live far enough north, Perseus can be seen every night. It will seem to run around Polaris. The Milky Way flows through Perseus from Cassiopeia. Algol seems to be brighter than Mirfak sometimes, but every two-and-a-half days it gets much dimmer. Algol is actually two stars. The dimmer one crosses in front of the brighter star, causing it to slowly "blink" for about ten hours. Perseus is a good place to see how sharp your starsight is. There is a beautiful double star cluster between Perseus and Cassiopeia, but it is hard to find because of the Milky Way. Use binoculars if you can get a pair.

Other Pointers

The Pleiades are a unique sight in the night sky. Many myths and stories have been told about them. The Pleiades are an "open cluster" of stars named after seven daughters of Atlas in Greek mythology. Most people see five bright stars. Steady binoculars will show up to fifty. These are mostly young stars — very blue and wispy.

A line from Algol through the Pleiades points to Taurus, home of the Hyades — another famous open cluster of new stars — and to Aldebaran. Aldebaran was an important star for the Indians because it told of the coming of summer. Two stars in the Pegasus square, Scheat and Markab, point south to a bright, but lonely "royal star," Fomalhaut. This star can only be seen in the Southern Hemisphere.

2

Sphere and Here

Where Is Here Anyway?

Everything in space moves — all of it rolls, tumbles, spins through time. Everything goes at its own direction and speed, all dancing together in time to celestial rhythms and harmonies.

Spinning is one way that spheres move. *Spheres* includes all stars, suns, planets, many moons, and earth. Spheres spin around an axis. On earth this axis is known as the North Pole at one end, and the South Pole at the other. These are not real poles, stuck into the ground, but it's nice to think of them that way, because you can easily picture earth spinning around a pole. On any sphere, these poles become the two most important reference points — especially for all navigation, exploration, and other travel. From these poles, you can start to tell every other direction.

A sphere spinning around its poles is rotating. Anyone on a rotating sphere is always moving. No matter if they're standing in one spot. On a sphere, anyplace you call "here" is never in one place for long.

Planets and asteroids move in long orbits around the sun. Other stars seem to have planets orbiting around them too, but they are very small and very far away, so it's hard to tell. Moons orbit around planets. Satellites orbit around moons and planets.

The sun is also moving around the center of the galaxy. And the galaxy seems to be moving too. But it's hard to tell exactly where it's all going or any other questions beyond that. We're too far away to know.

Any sphere orbiting around a central point is revolving. It takes the earth one year to make one complete revolution in its orbit around the sun. Knowing the night sky will become a lot easier when you first understand the two main ways the earth moves, and how this movement makes the stars seem to move.

Two Ways Spheres Move Around

Rotate means to spin or turn around an axis with a north pole and south pole.

One full rotation is one full *day* on earth. A record player turntable spins around an axis which is the spindle.

Revolve means to orbit around a central point. Planets revolve around the sun. Moons revolve around planets. The sun revolves around the galaxy. One revolution of the sun is one *year* on the earth. A quarter on a record player will revolve around the spindle, its axis, if it's running 45 rpm or slower. Orbits in our solar system spin counterclockwise when seen from above (the North Star).

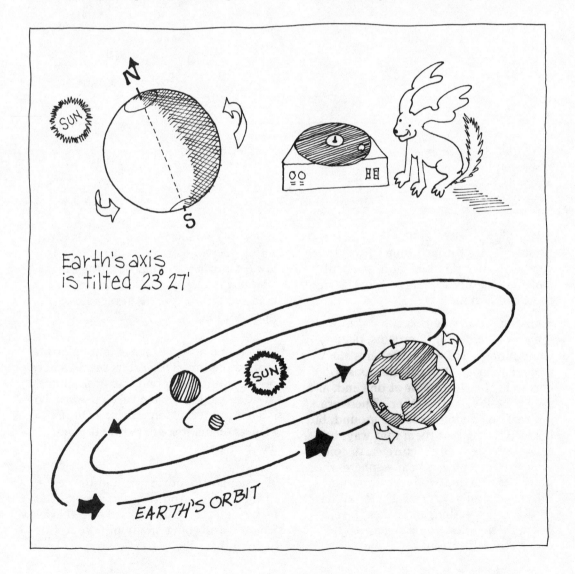

Earth's axis is tilted 23° 27'

EARTH'S ORBIT

Night Is Just a Strolling Shadow

Space is full of distant lights and darkness. Stars are glowing balls of gas that give off light in all directions. A beam of starlight will keep traveling through space unless there is something to bend it or bounce it into another direction. Something could be a planet, moon, spaceship, dust, or satellite. Otherwise the light keeps moving — farther from the star and getting dimmer and dimmer.

By the time starlight gets to earth, it is too dim to be seen in daytime. The sun is too bright. Try to cast a shadow of your hand with a flashlight onto a bright sunlit wall. You can't do it because the flashlight just isn't bright enough.

Night is the side of earth turned away from the bright sun. Night is a shadow. It's always there. But because the earth spins under it, we're only in the shadow of night about half the time. This shadow is what makes it possible for people to see the stars, and ask questions about them.

Knowing Light by Watching Shadows

Get a good flashlight and a couple of balls. Find a dark room. Figure out a way to hang the balls in the middle of the room. You can use strong twine or fishing line, and they don't have to be tied fancy as long as they hang so you can see them from all sides.

Imagine the room is the whole vast darkness of space. With your flashlight, you are the sun. In this solar system, a basketball can become the earth, and a softball can be the moon. Prop the flashlight up in one spot and go look at the globes. Is there a sharp or fuzzy line between "day" and "night" on the balls? Why do you think the sunset is called *twilight?*

Turn the globes slowly. Watch how the light hits them. Does the light cover more or less of the globe as you turn it? Are you sure? Hold one ball so it casts a shadow onto the other ball. Can you see how eclipses are caused?

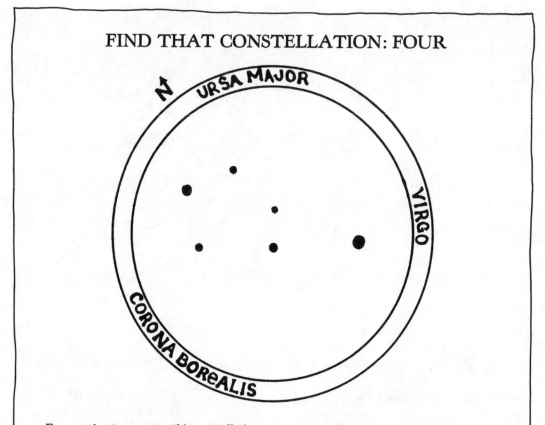

FIND THAT CONSTELLATION: FOUR

From spring to summer, this constellation will lead you right to the important stars that are known as the zodiac. It contains a very bright, giant star which has an orange glow. This is the key pointer star for finding the ecliptic this time of year.

Hint: In the old sky myths, he is the one who drives the Great Bear through the night.

Where to look for it: Begins to rise in the spring and grows higher in the sky during summer. Lasts until early autumn.

Answer on page 42.

Globes

The size and shape of a sphere is easier to understand if you can see and feel the whole globe. It's also easier to understand the earth's rotation when a globe is spinning in front of you.

Do you have a globe? New ones are nice, but they are sometimes expensive. You might be able to find a used globe at the Salvation Army or other thrift stores. One with latitude and longitude lines clearly printed on it is best. It's also nice to have one with the current names of all the countries. But it's OK to have an old globe with the old countries marked on it. The shapes of continents and coastlines change, but they don't change as fast as the names of countries do.

Your head is almost a globe — sort of. Imagine that the back of your head is night and your face and eyes are the daytime.

Patchwork World

Earth isn't perfectly round, all around. It's not an exact sphere shape. It's an *oblate spheroid*, which means that it's slightly flattened on top and bottom, at the poles. And it's slightly bulged in the middle, at the equator.

Most globes sold in stores are perfect spheres, and imperfect models of the earth. If you know how to sew, you can make a globe that is more accurate. It can be flat on top and bottom and slightly bulged in the middle, just like the real one. No globe will look and feel as good as one you make for yourself.

Make a Patchwork World

You can create a patchwork world out of fabric scraps. Start by making a pattern. Use a basketball for a model. Tape tissue paper onto it and trace the markings on the ball as close as possible.

You should have eight pieces of these shapes. They should fit together into one whole globe.

Round off the curves so the pieces match up right. You'll notice that the basketball isn't shaped exactly like these pieces. After you're sure that these will fit into a whole globe, make a second pattern on newspaper. This time add an extra ¼ inch along each edge. This will give you enough room to sew them all together.

Use this second pattern to mark and cut out on some muslin. Sew all but one of the strips together to make the shell of

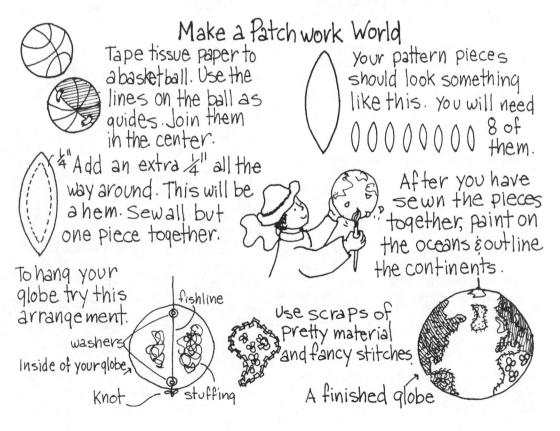

Make a Patchwork World

Tape tissue paper to a basketball. Use the lines on the ball as guides. Join them in the center.

Your pattern pieces should look something like this. You will need 8 of them. OOOOOOO

¼" Add an extra ¼" all the way around. This will be a hem. Sew all but one piece together.

After you have sewn the pieces together, paint on the oceans & outline the continents.

To hang your globe try this arrangement. fishline
washers
Inside of your globe,
Knot   stuffing

Use scraps of pretty material and fancy stitches.

A finished globe

the globe. Slip the shell around the ball and paint on the oceans using blue ink or watercolors. Also paint the one un-sewn strip. Leave swirls of white for clouds, if you want to. Remove the ball and sew on the last strip of the globe, but leave room to get your hand and the stuffing inside.

When you finish coloring the oceans, you are ready to select the right scraps for continents. Spend a lot of time choosing the right ones. Find patches that have earth colors (brown, red, green, blue, grey) that remind you of Africa, Europe, or South America. Whorls of white fabric can become clouds and storms.

Find a basketball-sized globe to use for tracing out patterns of the continents. If the globe is bigger or smaller than the ball you started with, you'll have to reduce or enlarge the continents in scale. Take time to select embroidery thread that looks nice and matches the patches. Now you're ready to appliqué the continents onto the globe. Pin them on first, if you're not sure how it will look.

Use shredded foam or kapok for stuffing. But before you stuff it, figure out how you're going to hang it. You can use two-pound-test fishline. Tie it to a pair of washers that run right through the axis of the globe.

When you stuff it, put more foam in the middle, so that the equator will bulge out. You can flatten the poles by hand, but they also get flatter after it hangs a while. If you're good at sewing, you can make your own best patchwork world. Or may-be you'll want to make earth pillows or another planet. You figure it out.

Gyroscopic Vision

A gyroscope is the skeleton of a globe — the running parts. Many new gyroscopes are made of plastic, so they aren't worth much. They make funny noises and they don't spin well. Try to find an all-metal gyroscope that spins smoothly.

To get the gyroscope started, you need to wrap the string carefully around the axis. Otherwise, it won't spin well. The loops of string should fit evenly, side by side, the way firemen wind up their hoses. You should be able to pull the string in one smooth, quick tug, without snagging it or otherwise hanging it up. Try to get the gyroscope spinning as fast as it can. Work at it, if you have trouble.

Gyroscopes are magic instruments. Get a good one and it will show you how the forces of gravity hold earth in its orbit. Earth isn't the same size as a gyroscope, and it moves at a different speed, but the forces are the same.

Be-It-Yourself Gyroscope

Keep your feet off the floor.

Do you know someone with a swivel chair or any other kind of seat that spins?

40

Perhaps they will let you use the chair to try this experiment. Do it, and you'll feel the powerful forces of a spinning gyroscope throughout your whole body.

Besides the chair, you'll need a bicycle wheel with an axle or something through it. This axle should allow the wheel to spin freely, without lots of friction to slow it down. You'll also need a friend to help out. Take turns in the chair, and you'll both feel these forces.

Sit with your feet off the floor. Hold the axle in both hands — straight out in front of you — so it spins as fast as it can. Ask your friend to start spinning the wheel

rapidly in a direction down and away from your chest.

Slowly turn the wheel to the right as it spins, until it is spinning on its side. What happens to you and the chair? Which way did you move? If the wheel is still spinning, turn it back to the left. Now what happens?

Ask your friend to start the wheel spinning in the other direction, toward your chest. Try the same things you did before. Slowly turn the wheel to the right, until it is again spinning on its side. Any change? Turn the wheel slowly in the other direction, until it is spinning on its other side. Now what happened?

Space in the Face of a Clock

Geometry is one kind of math that's very easy to see in everyday life. Buildings, houses, signs, or just about anything anyone builds could not be made without some understanding of geometry.

Space exists and moves according to the geometry of circles and angles. Don't worry if you haven't had geometry in school yet. The subject becomes a lot easier to understand once you stare into the face of a clock.

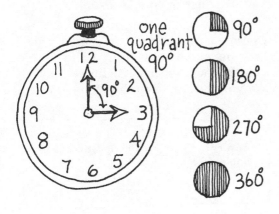

Our system of dividing circles into 360 degrees comes from ancient Chaldea. A circle of 360 equal parts can be divided into four quadrants, or quarter circles, having 90 degrees or three hours each. In other words, from noon to three is 90 degrees. From noon to midnight is 360 degrees. How many degrees are there in six hours?

A clock face is divided into 12 hours of 60 minutes each. How many degrees are there in one hour?

The number 360 is a magic number. Not many other numbers can be divided by as many whole numbers as 360. A total of 23 whole numbers can be divided into it without any remainder. Try dividing 360 by any of these numbers and see if anything is left over: 1, 2, 3, 4, 5, 6, 8, 9, 10, 12, 15, 18, 24, 30, 36, 40, 45, 60, 72, 90, 120, 180, 360.

This is also a convenient number to use because the earth's almost circular orbit is 365¼ days. This isn't exactly 360, but it's close enough. Then the year can be divided into four quadrants, which match the seasons.

Most early astronomy instruments and navigation devices had one thing in common. They were based on the circle and the system of dividing it into 360 equal degrees.

Circle Tools

Just about any art or school supply store has three tools you can use to understand circles and angles better. You've probably used them all before. One is a *ruler* with a good straight edge. The other is a *protractor*, which has angles for a half-circle measured out so it's easy to figure angles of altitude, latitude, clock hours, or pie pieces.

You can always draw a circle using a string and a pencil, of course. But you'll make a more accurate one if you get a circle *compass*. You will need these tools — or your own versions of them — to make many of the instruments and projects in this book.

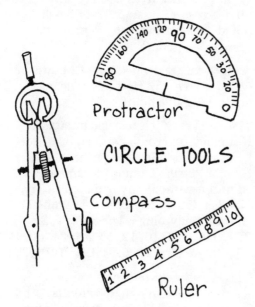

Protractor

CIRCLE TOOLS

Compass

Ruler

Handy Nadir-Zenith Finder

Nadir and zenith are two terms used in books on the stars. Everybody has a zenith and a nadir, even you. The zenith is the point directly over your head, no matter where on earth your head is at the time. The nadir is the point opposite your zenith — the lowest point — directly below your feet.

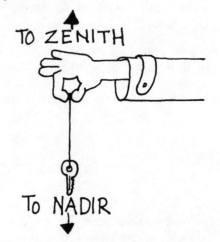

TO ZENITH

TO NADIR

If you have a string in your pocket, it's very easy to find your zenith and nadir. Just tie one end of the string onto something convenient, something that has a bit of weight: a key, a rock, a sinker, a nut, a bolt, anything. Just hold it out and when it stops swinging you've found the zenith and nadir.

What Is Your Horizon?

Everyone has a horizon, no matter where they are, or what time it is. Can you find yours? The horizon is the lowest spot of sky you can see. Your horizon always

Answer to Find That Constellation Four: Bootes (see map, page 50)

42

your Horizon

You can't see under here.

runs in a full circle all around you. Obviously some horizons are straighter and flatter than others. When you are at sea or in Kansas, the horizon is flat. When you are in western Colorado or Nevada, the horizon is jagged and jumbled by mountains.

It's easy to see how a horizon happens. Get a record and place it against any large ball. Imagine that you are standing on top of the record where the record hole touches the ball. Everything above the record in the sky would be visible to you. Everything over the edge of the

record would be invisible. The edge of a record all around would be the horizon, stretching to infinity. Where is the one place on a globe that you can see the whole night sky?   The equator.

Altitude and Stellar Elevations

To a pilot in an airplane, *altitude* means how high he is above the ground. To an astronomer or navigator on the ground, *altitude* means something else. To them, altitude is how high something is above the horizon. If you know where the horizon is, it's easy to find the altitude of a star, sun, or other object in the sky.

You can estimate the altitudes of things with your own two arms, almost the same way you estimate the angle of your field of view. Point one arm to the horizon. Point the other arm to the star or object. Hold your arms stiff and have a friend mark off the angle between your arms onto a big sheet of newspaper taped to the wall. Then use a protractor to figure the angle. This angle is the altitude of the object.

The altitude of one — and only one — star will also give you your latitude. Do you know which star this is? This is explained in the following pages.

How to Measure Altitude

Mark this angle.

To horizon

This angle is the altitude.

Horizon

(Use your protractor to measure the angle.)

Latitude and Polar Parallels

Early sailors and Greek thinkers knew the earth was sphere-shaped. Aristotle, the Greek wiseman, saw ships sail below the horizon and return. From a ship, coasts seem to "sink" below the horizon and then pop back up when the ship returns to port.

The Greeks invented the system we use for mapping globes. It works for all planets, moons, and other spheres besides earth. This system has lasted through the ages because it solves a problem that has always puzzled cartographers — people who make maps or charts. The problem is, how can you map something that has no corners?

All globes have no corners and only two "fixed" points to show directions: the North Pole and South Pole. These are where the Greeks decided to start the system. The system is simple. The whole globe is divided by two different kinds of lines — *latitude* and *longitude*.

Latitude measures how far you are from the equator, which is the longest line of latitude. It runs around the very middle of earth — halfway between both poles.

How to Tell Latitude by Altitude

On a clear night, it's always easy to find your latitude. Just measure the altitude of the North Star.

Lines of latitude are called *parallels*, because they all run parallel — side by side, without crossing. Parallels of latitude are numbered from the equator, which is 0 degrees. Parallels run north to the Pole, which is 90 degrees north latitude, and south to that pole, which is 90 degrees south latitude.

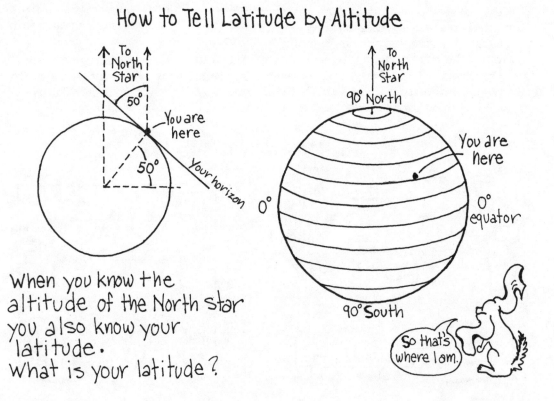

How to Tell Latitude by Altitude

When you know the altitude of the North star you also know your latitude.
What is your latitude?

44

FIND THAT CONSTELLATION: FIVE

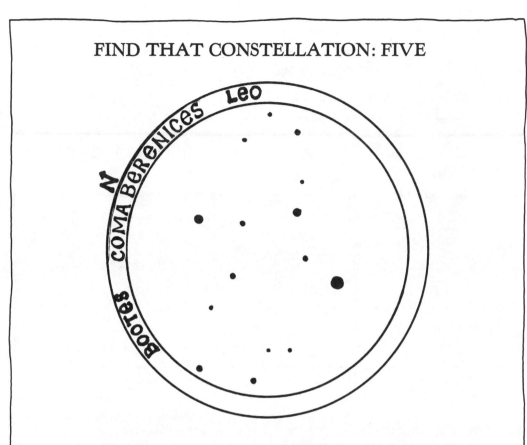

These stars outline the biggest constellation in the zodiac. It fills almost 50 degrees of the night skies in spring and summer.

Hint: This zodiac sign is not an animal. Many are in love with her.

Where to look for it: Begins rising in early spring and stays low on the southern horizon until late August.

Answer on page 46.

How High Is the Sky?

The Vikings' solar stone and the Polynesians' calabash were never as accurate as modern navigation instruments. Sticks stones, gourds, and other "crude" instruments have been replaced by more sophisticated ones. As people learn more about navigation, each new instrument becomes a little more accurate than the last. But just because an instrument is no longer used does not mean it is no longer valuable.

Modern navigators and travelers would probably never think of using an astrolabe or cross-staff, but these instruments aren't difficult to make. And they are accurate enough to help you find your way around the night sky. Or around the world!

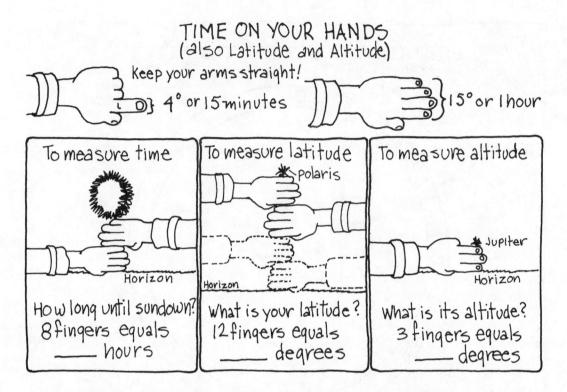

TIME ON YOUR HANDS
(also Latitude and Altitude)

keep your arms straight!

4° or 15 minutes

15° or 1 hour

To measure time

Horizon

How long until sundown? 8 fingers equals ___ hours

To measure latitude

polaris

Horizon

What is your latitude? 12 fingers equals ___ degrees

To measure altitude

Jupiter

Horizon

What is its altitude? 3 fingers equals ___ degrees

All Hands on Deck

Most early sailors and travelers could make a good guess at the altitude of the sun or a star. They simply stuck their arms out straight and started counting fingers — hand over hand from horizon to the sun or star. Many people also used this same method to figure out their latitude and to tell time.

This navigation technique involves a very simple estimate, but it's close enough for most folks. The sailors' standard hand is just the usual four fingers with the thumb tucked under. Four fingers are equal to about one hour of time, or 15 degrees of the 360 degree arc in a sky object's daily circle. Each finger is about 4 degrees, or 15 minutes of time.

All Hands Are Not Alike

Your hands may be smaller than the sailors' standard measure. Remember that this measurement was made by an old salty sailor. So measure yourself if you want to use this method.

One way to figure it out is to measure how many of your hands it takes to fill the 90 degrees between your horizon and zenith? Divide that number into 90 and find out how many degrees each hand is worth. One degree of arc is four minutes of time. Be sure to stick your arms out as far as you can each time you do this trick.

Cross-Staff

A cross-staff can look like a cross or a small *t* when it's not in use. But when it's used to sight a star, it looks more like a weapon from the Middle Ages.

Answer to Find That Constellation Five: Virgo (see map, page 50)

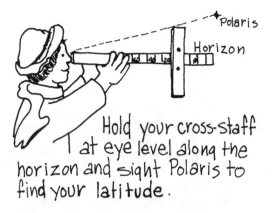

Hold your cross-staff at eye level along the horizon and sight Polaris to find your latitude.

Many sailors started using this simple instrument to measure latitude and altitude after it was introduced in 1325. It remained very popular and was used at sea for over 400 years by tradition-minded captains and navigators. More accurate instruments were invented during that time. These instruments were even used by Columbus and Captain Cook. But sailors still chose to use the cross-staff, because they knew it worked well.

In the late 1700s the cross-staff was finally replaced when sailors saw the advantages of newer instruments such as sextants and chronometers.

Make a Cross-Staff

It's easy to make a cross-staff. The only problem is finding an adequate connector, one that will slide up and down the staff, but will still hold both pieces of wood together.

Get three good pieces of lumber — 1x2 size. One piece should be six inches long, the next should be a foot long, and the third piece should be three feet long. You'll be able to get one longer piece and saw it.

If you look at the directions below, you'll see that in order to make a cross-staff, you need to make a holder for the long piece of wood to fit through. This holder is made by connecting the two smaller pieces together using carriage bolts. The holes should be far enough apart so that the other three foot piece can fit between them.

Make a Cross-Staff

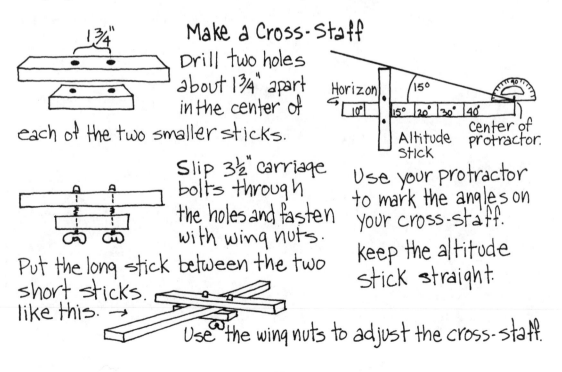

Drill two holes about 1¾" apart in the center of each of the two smaller sticks.

Slip 3½" carriage bolts through the holes and fasten with wing nuts.

Put the long stick between the two short sticks. like this. →

Use the wing nuts to adjust the cross-staff.

Use your protractor to mark the angles on your cross-staff.

keep the altitude stick straight.

47

Astrolabe

star

Try hanging your astrolabe from a tree or other steady support.

Astronomers and astrologers were using instruments like the astrolabe long before the first century A.D. But sailors didn't use the tool for navigation until 1,500 years later. The astrolabe wasn't very useful on small ships, because it couldn't be held steady. The tool be-came more useful at sea during the time of the larger and steadier clipper ships.

The astrolabe is an Arabic invention. It can be used to measure the same angles as the quadrant and cross-staff. This includes the altitudes of stars and other objects, and the latitude of the observer. A navigator using a special astrolabe and a timetable could also use the astrolabe to tell time.

How to Make a Simple Astrolabe

For the astrolabe wheel, use good wood or an old piece of round "junk" that looks good. Mark off *degrees of declination* all around the circle as in the illustration. Use wire or a band of something to hang it from. Then put a weight on the other end so it will hang straight down.

The astrolabe arm should be made of wood which is thick enough to cast a shadow. Attach the arm to the center of the wheel with a bolt, washers, and a wing nut.

Make Your Own Astrolabe

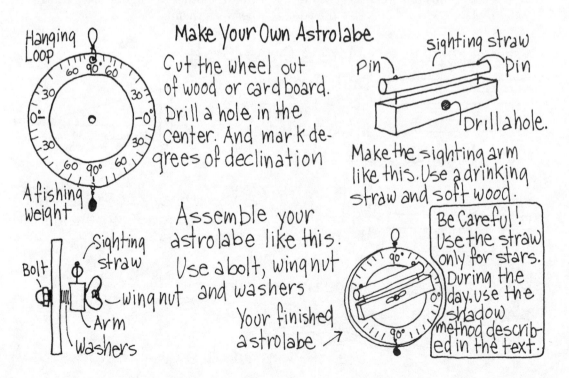

Hanging Loop

A fishing weight

Cut the wheel out of wood or cardboard. Drill a hole in the center. And mark degrees of declination

Bolt

Sighting straw

wing nut

Arm

Washers

Assemble your astrolabe like this. Use a bolt, wing nut and washers

Your finished astrolabe →

Pin

Sighting straw

Pin

Drill a hole.

Make the sighting arm like this. Use a drinking straw and soft wood.

Be Careful! Use the straw only for stars. During the day, use the shadow method described in the text.

Beware of Eye Damage

Remember this if you ever use an astro-labe to measure the altitude of the sun: Do not look straight into the sun when "sighting" it. This will damage your eyes. Use a shadow instead.

Make the instrument with a ½ inch thick wooden arm so it casts a good shadow. Hold the tool so sunlight creates the shadow above or below the arm. Move the arm until the shadow disappears. The arm should be pointing straight at the sun. This way you don't need to look at the sun, and you'll still be able to know its altitude.

FIND THAT CONSTELLATION: SIX

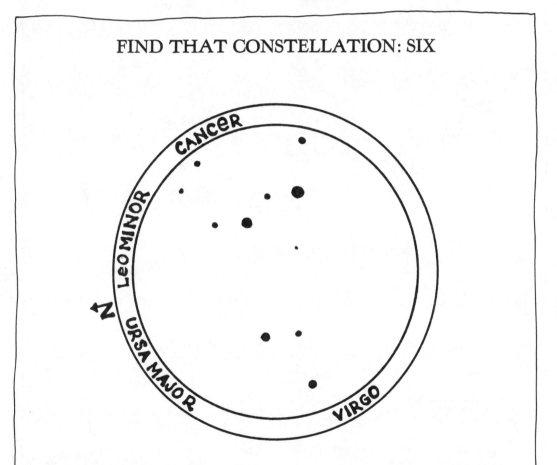

This constellation also belongs to the zodiac. Of all the star groups in the zodiac, this is one of the easiest animals to see in the sky. The animal's head looks like a question mark.

Hint: This is the only zodiac animal that you would expect to find in almost any zoo or circus.

Where to look for it: Begins rising in January and remains high in southern skies until July.

Answer on page 51.

49

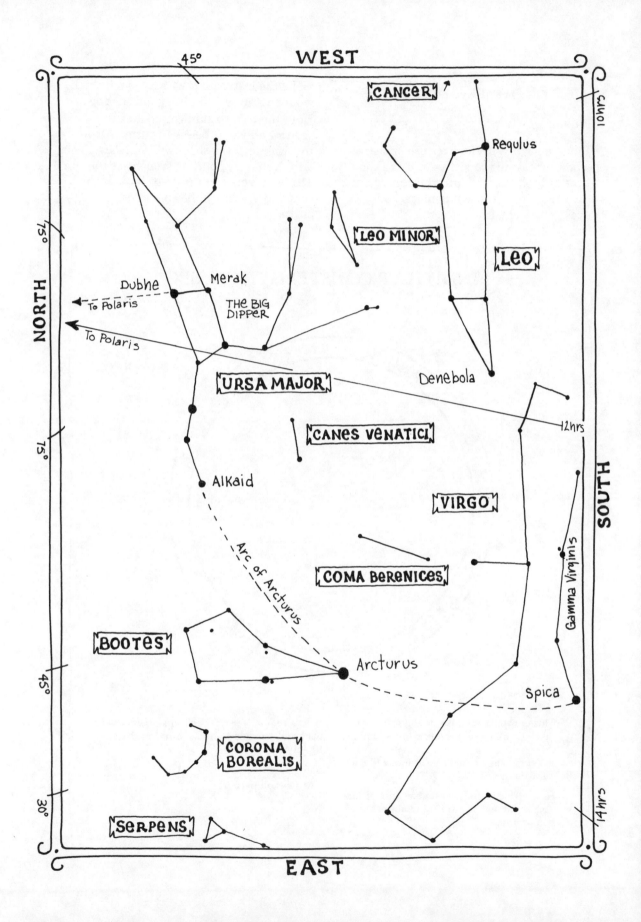

FIND THOSE CONSTELLATIONS: MAP TWO

All the stars in Find that Constellation games Four, Five, and Six can be found on this map. You can see these stars in the spring sky. They will be overhead at these times: late April (10 p.m.), late May (8 p.m.), and late June (6 p.m.).

These constellations will lead you to the middle of the zodiac during spring and summer. Each of them contains the brightest stars to be found in the night sky at this time of year. There aren't many other bright stars to confuse things in this part of the sky.

Bootes is the Bear Driver, or Herdsman. The ancients saw this kite-shaped constellation as the one that follows the Great Bear (Ursa Major) around the sky. Bootes contains a very bright, orange star, Arcturus. Arcturus is a giant star that can be found quickly, if you follow the curve of the Great Bear's tail or the handle of the Big Dipper, if that's how you see it. Continue this curve southward and it will lead you to another bright star, Spica, and to the next constellation.

Virgo is the Harvest Maiden. She is usually pictured with an ear of wheat in her hand. This stalk of wheat is called Spica, which is the brightest star in Virgo. Spica sits just below the ecliptic, the dividing line of the zodiac. Virgo moves through an empty part of the sky, and it is one of the longest constellations in the zodiac. Virgo was an important constellation to the ancients because it signaled the coming of the harvest. Spica is on the eastern horizon, behind the sun as it rises in mid-October, harvest time. Follow Spica westward along the zodiac and it will lead to Leo. Virgo also contains a fine double star, Gamma Virginis.

Leo, of course is the lion. A big and easy-to-spot constellation because it really looks like a resting lion — the stone ones that guarded doors and palaces in the days when statues were everywhere. The head of the lion looks like a question mark. It is called the Sickle. Leo's brightest star is Regulus, which means Prince. Regulus is the point at the bottom of the question mark. Near the tail of Leo is a triangle of bright stars. The brightest is Denebola, the tail of the lion.

Other Pointers

North of Virgo is a dim region of the sky known as Coma Berenices, the hair of Berenice. It's a hazy area between Leo and Bootes. It has very few stars and the constellation is hard to make out. Berenice must have had very fine hair! This area is good for binocular searches. It contains several star clusters. These are groups of wispy young stars, like those found in the Pleiades.

And in late spring, Spica points toward a bright star that is rising low on the horizon. This is Antares, a key star in the constellation Scorpius.

Answer to Find That Constellation Six:
Leo (see map, opposite)

3

Noon and Moon

The Wheel of Life

Everyone is a sign of the zodiac — Gemini, Leo, Aries, Scorpio, or something. Do you know yours? What else do you know about your sign? Where does your sign fit into the "Wheel of Life"? What does your sign have to do with the stars?

What Is the Zodiac?

Remember the large imaginary grapefruit movie screen — the one that all constellations seem to be projected upon? People call it the sky vault or celestial sphere. Across this celestial screen is a long, thin band of sky — a ring of special constellations.

This band is known as the zodiac. It stretches around in a full 360 degree circle, but is only about 17 degrees wide. It's easier to imagine if you've ever seen the wraparound cyclorama movies at Disneyland and world exposition fairs.

Zodiac is an old Greek word meaning "wheel of life." The 12 constellations that circle the zodiac are named after beings full of life: the Ram, the Bull,

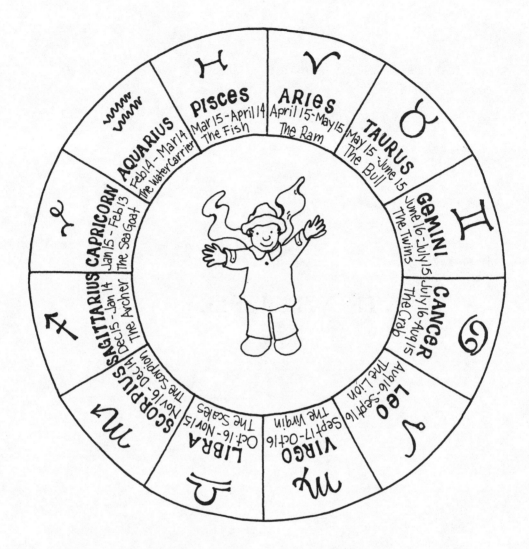

the Crab, the Lion, the Goat, the Fish. Each constellation covers 30 degrees of the full circle. Each constellation also has a sign in the zodiac. The signs or symbols for the constellations of the zodiac appear above.

Zodiac Tracks

Around the middle of the zodiac runs a line called the ecliptic. It's the path that the sun seems to take through the sky during the year. In summer the sun is high in the midday sky. It rises and sets in the northern latitudes. In winter the sun is low at midday and it rises and sets farther south.

The ecliptic changes every day. It marks the seasons. It's also the only place where eclipses happen. That's why it's called the ecliptic.

For many people, the zodiac is a great clock in the sky. The sun always rises in one of the 12 zodiac constellations. So do the moon and the other planets. Throughout the history of many lands, the zodiac has been the main way that many folks tell time.

FIND THAT CONSTELLATION: SEVEN

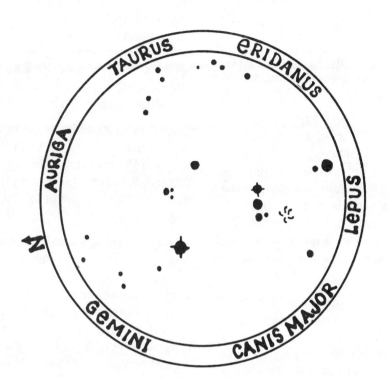

This is one of the most outstanding constellations. In ancient myths it is closely associated with five other constellations around it, a bull, two dogs, a rabbit, and a unicorn.

Hint: Some call him the hunter and some call him a giant.

When to look for it: Starts rising after Christmas and dominates winter skies to the south. It remains visible until spring.

Answer on page 58.

Astronomy: Science of Seconds

The early Greek view of the universe was a lot like the Navajo Indian view. The Greeks thought the universe was like an onion, a big bulging thing with lots of different worlds, each with a different layer. Plato, the ancient Greek wise man, said that what leads people from one of these worlds to the next is astronomy.

Astronomy is the scientific study of stars, suns, moons, planets, space — all together. At the center of astronomy is the study of earth, because earth is our first viewpoint.

Someone who studies this science is an astronomer. They use many exact instruments, including many kinds of telescopes, spectroscopes, satellites, and other machines. Astronomy is an exact science. It involves the very precise measurement of tiny fractions of seconds.

Astrology: Craft of Old

Astrology is an ancient sky-reading craft that is actually two separate studies — *natural* and *judicial.*

Natural astrology is about telling time. It's a very old craft based on careful observation and record keeping. Natural astrologers draw up calendars, keep track of seasons, predict eclipses, and chart the phases and signs of the moon, planets, and other objects in the solar system. This kind of astrology is about time. Many people believe it is a grandparent of astronomy.

Judicial astrology is interested in telling stories. It's sometimes called mundane astrology. Mundane means commonplace. A lot of judicial astrology is commonplace because it makes broad general "predictions" and "horoscopes" about people's future — mostly their money and love problems. For many people this kind of astrology is great fun and games. For others it is just plain boring.

Astrology has helped people learn how to tell time and keep accurate calendars. But much that is now said and written about the old craft is clouded in mysterious language. The words try to describe things that are hard to picture, measure, or explain well. Many modern astronomers don't believe a word of astrology because of this.

Answer to Find That Constellation Seven: Orion (see map, page 72)

What's "in Gemini"?

Sun, moon, planets, and other space wanderers are best located against the background of a constellation. The sun can be located by noting the constellation behind it when it rises and when it sets. The same is true for Jupiter or Mars or any other "nearby" celestial object.

This is what astronomers are talking about when they say the sun is "in Gemini," and Saturn is now "in Sagittarius." The constellation is seen behind the planet, like the curtain behind a singer on stage.

Astrologers mean something else when they say the sun is "in Gemini." Astrologers talk about signs, not constellations. They mean the sun rises in the sign of Gemini, a slice of the zodiac which is 30 degrees long. Actually, the sun would be seen rising in front of Taurus. Gemini, the constellation, has moved back from that spot in the sky since the astrologers' system began long ago.

This book aims to help you observe the sky, so when it says a planet is "in" something, it means the planet is "in" front of the constellation, not the sign. It wouldn't make sense to search for the object in the wrong place.

Ring Around the Zodiac

You can use 3" x 5" cards to learn the signs of the zodiac. These cards are close to the scale and dimensions that each sign holds in the sky, 30 degrees by 17 degrees.

Make 12 cards, one for each sign. On one side of the card, write the symbol and draw the stars and constellation for each sign. On the other side, write the name and symbol for the stars.

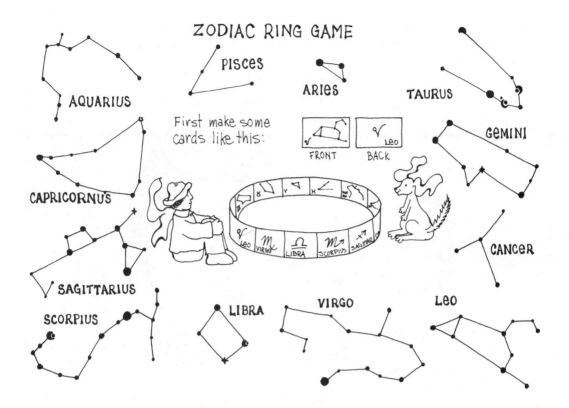

ZODIAC RING GAME

PISCES

ARIES

TAURUS

AQUARIUS

GEMINI

First make some cards like this:

FRONT   BACK

CAPRICORNUS

CANCER

SAGITTARIUS

VIRGO   LEO

SCORPIUS   LIBRA

Tape all the cards together in the right order in a ring. Put the drawings of the constellations on the inside of the ring. Make sure all the right cards and right sides match up. Put the sun — an orange, lemon, or something — in the middle of this circle.

When your zodiac is complete, it should look like the one above.

Zodiac Ring Game

You can use the zodiac ring for a rainy day board game. Sit with the zodiac ring between you and a friend. Roll dice to see who starts. Whoever begins must name the constellation straight across from where he or she sits. If the person does it, he or she must name any date when the constellation is on the horizon at sunrise. Each correct answer leads to a new turn. Use the chart on page 56 to help you figure out the dates for each constellation, or write them on the backs of the cards ahead of time. First one to complete the zodiac circle is the winner.

One Smartaleck Trick

"Hi. What's your sign?" The next time anyone asks you this dumb question do this: Draw the stars and constellation of your sign in the dirt, sand, or on a piece of paper. Show it to the person who asked the question.

Wait for a reaction. Then, if they don't know, draw the symbol for the constellation. Wait for another reaction. Then if they still don't know, you can decide if you want to tell them or not.

What *is* your sign? Do you know what the constellation looks like?

FIND THAT CONSTELLATION: EIGHT

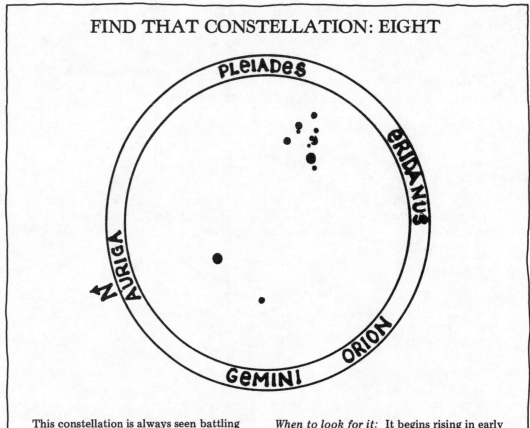

This constellation is always seen battling with another group of nearby stars. It contains two important clusters of young stars and a very famous crab-shaped cloud. It is a member of the zodiac family.

Hint: This big-horned animal can be found on the farm or at the rodeo.

When to look for it: It begins rising in early December. One of the bright constellations of winter, it sets in spring.

Answer on page 62.

The Problem of Longitude

Sailors and other travelers have been measuring latitude for at least 2,000 years. When they wanted to find how far north of the equator they were, all they needed was a clear night, and a way to measure the altitude of Polaris.

But finding longitude was and still is a problem because the lines of longitude aren't parallel. They all meet at the

North and South Poles, like spokes meet at the middle of a wheel. This means that degrees of longitude are not the same width, especially as you get closer to either pole.

Most early sailors navigated like the Polynesians who used the calabash to find Hawaii. They sailed straight north or south until they found the right latitude for their destination. Then they would turn 90 degrees and sail east or west, until they got to where they were going. This took them way out of the way. No wonder early travel was so difficult!

Earth on a Turntable

What if each record you bought had the hole in a different spot on the record? Wouldn't hear much music would you? This is like another problem sailors had with longitude.

No one on earth could agree where to begin the system of longitude, so each nation picked its own spot. Usually each nation's capital city became its 0 degree line. Everybody used a different system, and it was very confusing.

After the invention of the chronometer in 1761, the problem still wasn't solved. The chronometer helped navigators make exact measurements of time and longitude

from a certain starting point. But, again, everyone had a different starting point.

Almost 125 years passed before all the nations got enough together to end this nonsense. In 1884 they agreed to set the zero spot at the Royal Greenwich Observatory, in London. This established the Greenwich Prime Meridian.

The Midday Lines

Any day, anywhere on earth, the sun will reach its zenith somewhere in the sky. This is known as noon or midday. This instant each day marks your meridian. *Meridian* means "midday line." Meridians of longitude are drawn in big circles through both poles and around the globe. Meridians are all the same length.

On one side of earth, a meridian is 12 hours ahead of the other half — going west. In other words, at 3 p.m. on one side of the meridian, it's 3 a.m. on the other side.

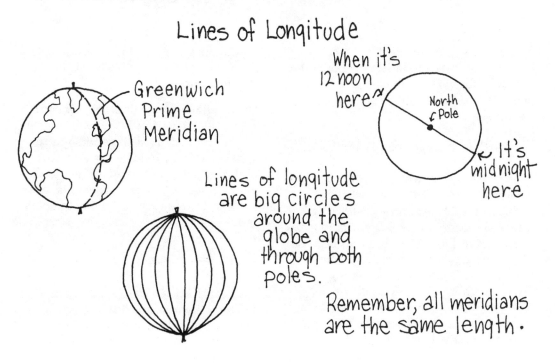

Lines of Longitude

Greenwich Prime Meridian

When it's 12 noon here

North Pole

It's midnight here

Lines of longitude are big circles around the globe and through both poles.

Remember, all meridians are the same length.

Making a Basketball Earth

Find a basketball and mark the lines of latitude and longitude.
Remember, latitude lines are parallel circles of different sizes. Longitude lines are all the same length.

Lines of Latitude

Lines of Longitude

One way people tell the difference between longitude and latitude: Longitude lines are always the same length. Parallels of latitude are always circles of different sizes.

Earth in the Face of a Basketball

An old basketball will show how any sphere is marked with a crisscrossing system of latitude and longitude. You can also use any other large round ball for this, but basketballs are best because they are already partly marked. Just be sure it is OK to mark the ball you use some more. A basketball will already have lines on it. On this imaginary earth, these are the longitude lines — sort of. All the lines — not just two —

should cross at the "poles" of the ball for it to look exactly like longitude. But it's close enough.

Do you have a large dark felt-tip pen? Mark the parallels of latitude on the ball. These circles start at the middle of the sphere (which would be the equator), and they get smaller as they get closer to the poles. They are always spaced the same distance apart. To make the parallels, use some string to line up each circle before you mark it.

Answer to Find That Constellation Eight: Taurus (see map, page 72)

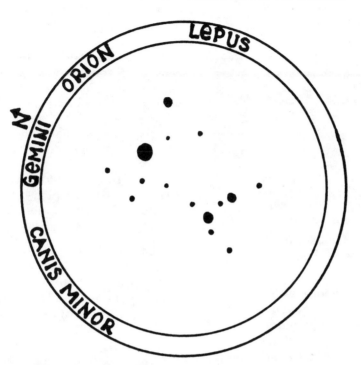

The brightest star known on earth can be found in this southern hemisphere constellation. It looks a lot like the animal it's named after. Nearby is another constellation named after the same creature.

Hint: This animal does not belong to the zodiac, but it's the Hunter's best friend.

When to look for it: It's always low in the southern sky as seen from North America. In some places it can be seen in January. It stays low during the winter and sets in early spring.

Answer on page 66.

Time Diggers and Time Tellers

An archeologist digs through time, trying to learn about ancient people from the things they left behind, either buried in the ground or just scattered around. In recent years archeologists have been working with astronomers to learn more about what the ancients knew of their place on earth and among the stars. Together they have formed a new science known as astro-archeology.

British astronomer Gerald S. Hawkins is a founder of the new science. Hawkins was one of the first to prove that Stonehenge, the great stone circle in England, was a kind of sky clock. With the aid of a computer, Hawkins found that Stonehenge was used to tell the changing of the seasons and to predict future eclipses.

Astro-archeologists have discovered some-

thing important. All over the globe, ancient people were familiar, fascinated, and preoccupied with the sky — night and day.

Priests and other religious leaders gained great power when they could correctly predict an eclipse or the beginning of flood season. In those times, food supplies depended on accurate charting and watching of the sky. As modern people look back across centuries, Stonehenge and other sky monuments seem to be big mysteries or big mistakes. Some people believe that the ancients were helped by know-it-all astronaut-gods, beings who came down from the sky in spaceships.

Modern people have trouble understanding ancient people's appreciation of the sky. Mostly because modern people don't know the sky very well. This cuts people off from a simple truth. In the old days, ancient people knew the stars the way you know the streets of your neighborhood.

Anywhere Sundial

Pick up any stick, hold it out, and you have a sundial. It will give a rough estimate of the time of morning and afternoon.

Stick the stick between your thumb and first finger. Hold your palm out flat so the stick makes a shadow. In the morning use your left hand and point the fingers west. In afternoon use your right hand and point the fingers east. In both cases the stick should point to the north. Tilt the stick so that the shadow is long enough to fill your whole hand, out to the finger tips.

Where is the shadow now? Would this work on a cloudy day? Why?

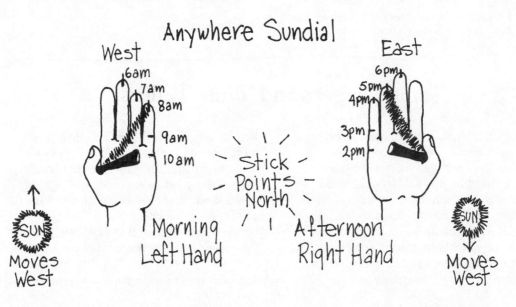

Anywhere Sundial

Night Clock

Many people see Polaris as the center of a great night sky clock. A few old sailors and sky gazers were experienced enough to tell time by sighting Polaris and the constellations around it. In the 16th century their experience was the basis for a new time-telling instrument, the night clock.

It isn't hard to make your own night clock. For best results, you should use plywood and paint. You could use cardboard too, but it won't last long. After you decide what to use, carefully trace

out and number the three pieces according to the pattern given in the diagram.

Wait until the patterns are completely dry, then cut them out. All three fit together at the holes in the middle. Drill holes big enough so a fastener just fits through all three. The best fastener is one that has a hole in it, so you can sight the North Star. Take the three pieces of wood to a hardware store and get a short piece of thin pipe. Make sure the pipe has threads on both ends, so you can use two nuts to fasten it all together. Here are patterns for the three pieces of the night clock.

A Pattern for a Night Clock

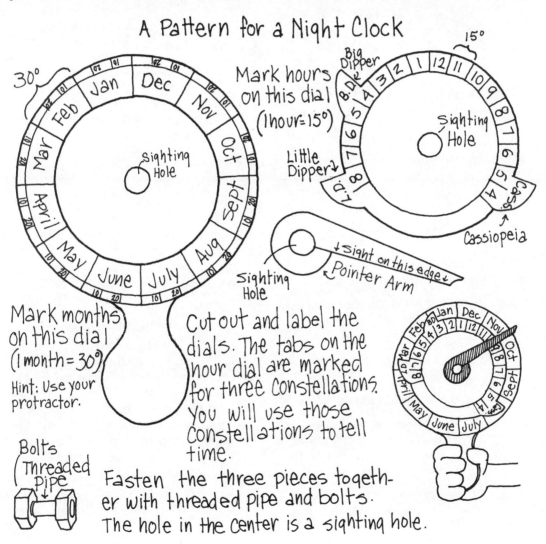

Mark hours on this dial (1 hour = 15°)

Little Dipper↓

Big Dipper

Sighting Hole

Cassiopeia

Sighting Hole

Sight on this edge↓
Pointer Arm

Sighting Hole

Mark months on this dial (1 month = 30°)

Hint: Use your protractor.

Cut out and label the dials. The tabs on the hour dial are marked for three constellations. You will use those constellations to tell time.

Bolts
Threaded Pipe↓

Fasten the three pieces together with threaded pipe and bolts. The hole in the center is a sighting hole.

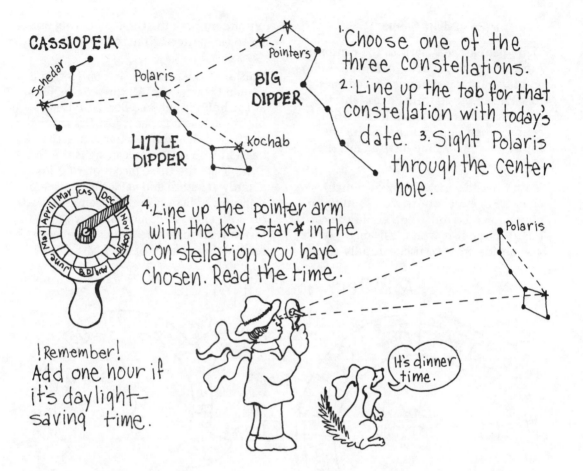

CASSIOPEIA

Schedar

Polaris

BIG DIPPER

Pointers

LITTLE DIPPER

Kochab

1. Choose one of the three constellations. 2. Line up the tab for that constellation with today's date. 3. Sight Polaris through the center hole.

4. Line up the pointer arm with the key star✳ in the constellation you have chosen. Read the time.

Polaris

! Remember! Add one hour if it's daylight-saving time.

It's dinner time.

How to Use the Night Clock

After you find Polaris, it's easy to use this night clock. Here's how:

1. Find one of these three constellations — Cassiopeia, Ursa Minor, or Ursa Major — in the sky.

2. Find the tab for this constellation on the hour dial.

3. Line up the tab with today's date.

4. Find the North Star through the hole in the dial. If the fastener doesn't have a hole, try to line the star up straight behind the center of the dials.

5. Line up the pointer arm to the key star in the constellation you picked (see drawing).

6. Read the time from the hour dial, and adjust for daylight-saving time if it's summer. The pointer should be pointing to the correct hour on the dial.

How Daylight-Saving Time Changes Charts

Hours on this and most other sky clocks are told in standard time. But in summer most of the United States uses daylight-saving time, or DST. Clocks on DST are set one hour ahead of standard time, so that people can have more evening day-

Answer to Find That Constellation Nine: Canis Major (see map, page 72)

light for work and play. If DST is being used (May to October), add one hour to the times you read off the night clock dial.

Lunar Sticks and Lunar Bones

Each month the moon almost dies. But not quite. It's reborn just in time to start life all over. After a couple of days of no moon, the moon is seen as a thin sliver in the evening sky. For 13 nights, it grows until it reaches its fullest face. This is celebrated with 3 nights of dancing. One night for each of three moons — full, strong, healthy.

Then the moon begins to die again. For the next 13 nights, the great hunter (the sun) battles the moon. And slowly slices it away, until there is no moon. It seems to be dead for a couple of days, but it's not. The moon never dies.

This is how the Bushmen of South Africa explain the story of the moon's monthly phases to people who don't know it. Archeologists know Bushmen are fascinated by the moon, because they mark its monthly changes on bones, sticks, and cave walls.

Faces of the Moon

After the sun, the most obvious time-teller in the sky is the moon. The moon's face goes through definite changes of expression each month. Actually it takes 29 days, 12 hours, and 44 minutes for the moon to complete one orbit as seen from the earth. This is known as the moon's phases, or the synodic month.

In each box, draw how the moon looks from earth during its four big changes. (If this is not your book, draw these on another piece of paper.)

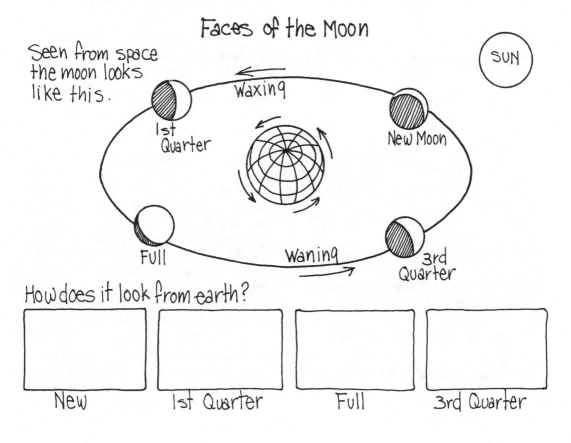

Faces of the Moon

Seen from space the moon looks like this.

SUN

Waxing

1st Quarter

New Moon

Full

Waning

3rd Quarter

How does it look from earth?

New	1st Quarter	Full	3rd Quarter

Do-It-Yourself Moon Bone

Get a good stick or a big piece of bone, one you can hold in your hand. Also get a hand knife, screwdriver, or something else to chip the bone.

Find the date of the next new moon. Check an almanac, the weather bureau, or a newspaper. Start marking the bone at the new moon, which is also the time of no moon. Make a small deep dot for no moon.

For the next few evenings watch as the moon increases in size. This is the waxing moon. Notice how it looks each night until it becomes full. Try to carve each night's moon on the bone just the way it looks in the sky. Keep marking it each night as the moon starts to wane and finish one phase.

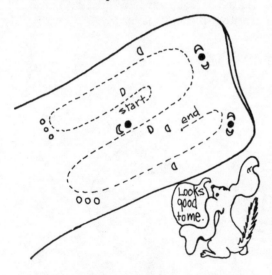

Look at this moon bone. Two phases of the moon are marked on it. Can you tell where new moons, full moons, quarter moons are marked?

Questiohs for a Moon Bone

How long did the moon take to go through one phase? This is the number of nights in one "moon."

Did you notice any changes in earth life as the moon went through its monthly change? If so, what were they?

Mayan Calendar

Songs and dim recollections are about all that most early cultures have to tell of their beginnings. The origin of modern cultures isn't always certain, either. Some scholars now believe Christ was born in 7 B.C. — seven years "before Christ"! So our whole calendar may be off.

In Mexico the ancient Mayan Indians were not at all confused about the date of their origins. For them, time began in 3114 B.C., because this is when their calendar began. No one argues with the Mayan calendar.

The Maya were spellbound by time. Their calendar is more accurate than those we know now, because it was based on exact sky observations and careful tracking of the sun, moon, and planets — especially Venus. Mayan priests kept complete almanacs that predicted eclipses and adjusted for leap years. Mayan almanacs of the orbit of Venus were only 14 seconds off for a whole year!

To the Maya, time was a relay race. They saw the sky as full of gods who ran at different speeds as they carried the weight of time around the heavens. These carrier gods changed with each day, year, decade, century. Priests knew how the gods moved, because they kept the calendar. The calendar held the key to their religion.

Your Own Calendar

Ever thought about making your own calendar? You can use your own numbering system, like the Maya. Or you can use the one that most of the world now uses, the Gregorian calendar. No calendar will be helpful if you can't read it and easily translate it into Gregorian calendar days. Leave enough blank space around each date so that you can write down your plans for that day or anything else that actually happens then.

Give each month a picture. NASA, the space agency, prints many booklets with fantastic color pictures of the earth, sun, moon, planets, rockets, stars. These booklets don't cost much. You can order them from the nearest U. S. Government Printing Office Bookstore (see the phone book).

Or you can send for a list of NASA publications from:

Office of Public Affairs
National Aeronautics and Space
Administration
Washington, D. C. 20546

Other things you might want to include on your calendar: dates of solstices, equinoxes, moon phases, meteor showers, eclipses, and positions of special planets. Just follow the example set by the Maya. Make it accurate.

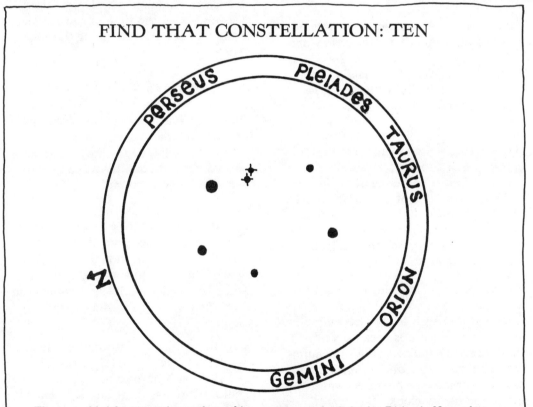

FIND THAT CONSTELLATION: TEN

The second brightest star in northern skies is located in this constellation. Some Americans see this star as a football sailing over the "uprights." Near this bright star is one so dark you can't see it!

Hint: In mythology this character sometimes drove a chariot and other times herded goats.

When to look for it: Rising in November, these stars are directly overhead for most of North America during the winter months. The constellation sets in late spring.

Answer on page 70.

The Medicine Wheels

Today the North American Great Plains are covered with countless circles of stone, circles that most archeologists call teepee rings. Some scientists estimate that there are five million rings across the plains from Texas to Canada. But that's only a guess.

There's nothing special about these stone circles, scientists say. Indians simply used stones to hold down their teepees, which were round at the bottom. But there are a few stone circles on the Great Plains that confound the scientists, as well as the Indians!

Indians who now live near the circles say "the sun built them" or "they were here when we came." Indians call the circles "medicine wheels." Until lately, nobody knew exactly who built them or how they were used.

One of these "wheels" may measure over 100 feet across — too large to be useful as the base of a teepee. Some wheels have 28 "spokes" crossing at a pile of rocks in the middle of the circle. Most wheels have other lines which shoot off from the main circle into different directions on the eastern horizon, as if they were pointing at something.

For centuries the meaning of all these lines was a big mystery until a few astro-archeologists began to study them. Some scientists were curious because a few wheels have 28 spokes — the same number of days as a "moon," or an Indian month. Perhaps the medicine wheel was some kind of sky clock.

The scientists began using modern instruments to check the alignments of rocks around and through the wheel. Their careful study showed that the rocks are indeed pointing at something: the sun and three stars — Aldebaran, Rigel, and Sirius. These are the three brightest compass stars rising at dawn at that time of year.

Furthermore, everything about the medicine wheels seemed to point toward one special day, the summer solstice. For the month before and after the solstice, one of the stars can be found before sunrise on the eastern horizon. The places where these stars rise are clearly marked around the wheel.

For the Plains Indians, the solstice was a big event. They knew it was the time when the sun is highest in the sky and the "growing power" of the world is strongest. Medicine wheels were used, it seems, to set the time of summer ceremonies and events, including the sun dance.

Your Own Medicine Wheel

Do you live near the Rocky Mountains or western Great Plains? Maybe there are old medicine wheels in your area. Can you find them? If you can't find one, maybe you can make one.

Do you know a place that would make a good secret spot for a medicine wheel? A field or flat place on a hill will do well. Any place you pick should have a good view of the horizon and lots of rocks. And of course, you must get permission from the owner of the land before you use it.

Start this project in late spring, when the stars are right. First lay out the circle. It doesn't have to be big. Maybe a natural circle is there already. Pile up a few stones to mark the circle's center.

Answer to Find That Constellation Ten: Auriga (see map, page 72)

Early one morning in late May, go to the circle before sunrise. Invite friends along if you want help. Before the sun comes up, stand at a spot on the northwest rim of the circle. This is the star-viewing spot. The first star you're looking for is Aldebaran, in the constellation of Taurus. Can you find it?

After you're sure you've found Aldebaran, mark your star-viewing spot on the western rim of the circle with a pile of rocks. Then pile up rocks to mark the spot on the rim where Aldebaran seems to rise.

Do the same rock markings later for the stars Rigel and Sirius. Sight each of them from the same star-viewing spot. And mark the point where each star touches the eastern rim of the circle. Rigel will be rising in Orion about a week before the solstice. Sirius, the brightest star, will be rising in Canis Major about a month after the solstice.

On the morning of the solstice (usually June 21, but check an almanac to be sure), go to the circle and stand on the southwest rim. Look northeast. When the sun starts to come up, move along the rim until the rock pile in the circle's center stands between you and the rising sun. Mark the spot on the rim where you're standing. Then mark the point on the other side of the rim where the sun seems to be touching it.

You will be marking sight lines just like the builders of the medicine wheels did. These alignments of sun and stars along the circle will be clearer after you study the medicine wheel layouts.

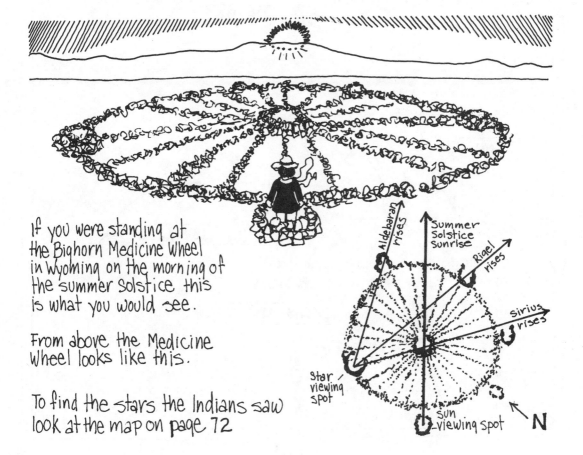

If you were standing at the Bighorn Medicine Wheel in Wyoming on the morning of the summer solstice this is what you would see.

From above the Medicine Wheel looks like this.

To find the stars the Indians saw look at the map on page 72

Aldebaran rises

Summer Solstice Sunrise

Rigel rises

Sirius rises

Star viewing spot

Sun viewing spot

N

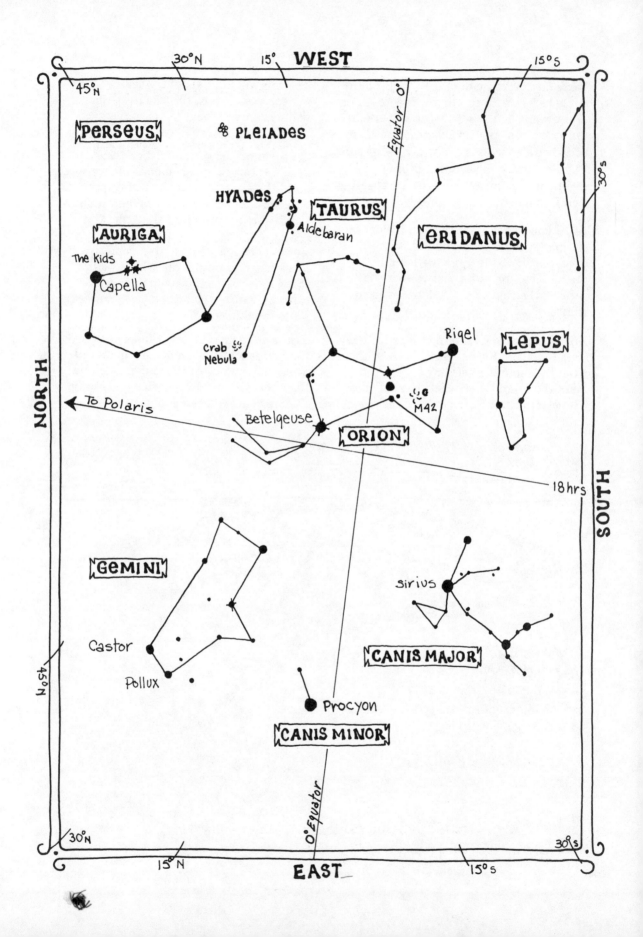

FIND THOSE CONSTELLATIONS: MAP THREE

Find That Constellation games Seven, Eight, Nine, and Ten are answered on this map. You can see these stars in the winter sky. They will be overhead at these times: late January (10 p.m.), late February (8 p.m.), late March (6 p.m.).

This portion of night sky contains all three of the Indian medicine wheel stars and some of the best-defined constellations and brightest stars you'll ever see all at once in northern skies. All of these are best viewed in midwinter when they stand out above the southern horizon. The Greeks saw Orion as a hunter followed by his two dogs (Canis Major and Canis Minor). Orion is running right over a rabbit (Lepus) to battle with the Bull (Taurus). Two bright constellations, Auriga and Gemini, are near this celestial battleground. But they aren't part of the action. Auriga seems to have enough action of his own.

Orion is the Hunter. It's the brightest winter constellation and one of the most spectacular, partly because you don't have to stretch your neck to see it. In most of North America, it dominates the southern horizon. Rigel and Betelgeuse (an obvious red supergiant) are the brightest stars in this constellation. The three stars of Orion's belt are located just below the celestial equator. The belt is a good way to locate the middle of the sky. Near these stars is a great cloudy nebula of gas. To unaided eyes this nebula can be seen as a blur around Orion's sword.

Taurus, the Bull, is a member of the zodiac family. Two of the most famous night sky objects are found in Taurus: the Crab Nebula and the Pleiades. The Crab Nebula is an expanding gas cloud, also known as M1. Over 6,000 light years away, this is all that remains of the Chi-nese "Guest Star" of 1054 A.D. At that time, this star became so bright, it could be seen in daylight! But now you're lucky if you can see it with unaided eyes. In binoculars held steadily, the nebula is a smudge to sharp eyes. The Pleiades are a bright cluster of young stars located on the shoulder of the bull. A less brilliant cluster is the Hyades. Across from them is Aldebaran, the seventh brightest star in the northern sky. Aldebaran is the bull's eye!

Canis Major is Orion's Big Dog. It looks very much like the animal it's named for. Canis Major contains Sirius, the brightest star any earthling can see. Egyptians worshipped Sirius and called it the "Dog Star." By waiting for Sirius to rise on the morning horizon, ancient Egyptian priests would foretell the yearly overflowing of the Nile River. Their food supply depended on knowing when the river would rise to irrigate the fields. Some people claim Sirius is so bright, it can be seen in daytime, if you know where to look and use a telescope.

Auriga is the Wagon Driver. Some old atlases call it the Goat Herder, but that's confusing because Capricorn is the Sea Goat in the zodiac. Think of it as a football goal post with the second brightest northern star, Capella, zooming through the uprights! South and west of Capella is a small triangle of stars known as "the Kids." One is a normal sun, but the other two are bizarre stars. Where earthlings only see these two stars, there are actually four. One of these is so big it would swallow earth, if it were centered where the sun is. Another would blind us if it were our sun, and we wouldn't even be able to see the third. In fact, it's invisible everywhere. It's an infrared star producing light rays so long that people can't see them.

Planets and Orbits

Bare-Eye Astronomy

Most people can see about 2,000 stars in the whole night sky, without using binoculars, telescopes, or any other sky-magnifying aids. With their own two eyes, some people can see stars as dim as seventh magnitude, depending on the seeing conditions. People can also see five planets with unaided eyes.

Magnitudes

As night falls, the brightest planets and stars come out first. How do people tell if a star is brighter or dimmer than another star? By their magnitudes.

Magnitude is the common measurement of a star's or planet's brightness. Bright objects have magnitude numbers that are small (1.2 or -0.9). Dim objects have big magnitude numbers (5.5 or 14.3).

Sirius, the brightest star, has a magnitude of -1.6. Sirius is brighter than Canopus, magnitude -0.9. Canopus is brighter than Spica, 1.2 magnitude. Jupiter has a magnitude of -2.5. Is Jupiter brighter or dimmer than Sirius?

With unaided eyes, most people can see magnitudes as dim as 4 or 5. Others can see fainter ones, especially if they know how to *not look* for them!

Now You See It, Now You Don't

Gaze into the night sky for a minute. Don't focus your eyes on anything, just let your attention drift to any bright star that catches your eye. Stop and focus on that star.

While you're looking at the bright star, you'll probably notice several dim stars on the edge of your vision. Don't look straight at any of them — not until you get a feeling for where one of them is.

Now look at it. What happened? It probably disappeared. Just as soon as you stared at it. Look away, back at the original bright star. Did the dim disappearing star come back? It should have, unless you looked straight at it again.

What's going on? Some observant people see stars of sixth and even seventh magnitude, but only in their side vision. Stars below fourth magnitude will usually disappear when you start to stare at them, but they appear to come back

out once you look away. This happens because there is a "blind spot" on the retina of everyone's eyes. This is the place where the optic nerves connect with the inside of the eye. This spot is not sensitive to very dim light.

So, if you ever want to see a dim star — don't look *at* it! Look *around* it, and it will pop into view.

When Is a Star Up?

Why do some stars stay hidden for part of the year? Why do other stars never set? Imagine that you are facing north. These diagrams will help you figure out the answers to these and maybe other questions.

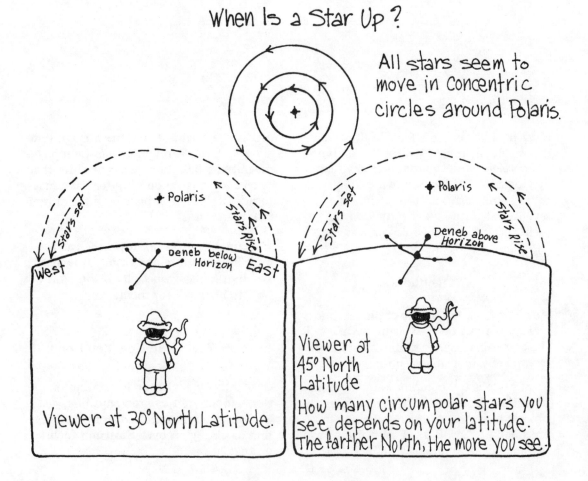

When Is a Star Up?

All stars seem to move in concentric circles around Polaris.

Polaris

Stars set · Stars Rise

West — Deneb below Horizon — East

Viewer at 30° North Latitude.

Polaris

Stars set · Stars Rise

Deneb above Horizon

Viewer at 45° North Latitude. How many circumpolar stars you see depends on your latitude. The farther North, the more you see.

Time-Lapse Photos

Astronomers use cameras to see far beyond what eyes can see. Photography can stretch time out. It can draw stars out of darkness, way beyond magnitudes that an astronomer can see through a telescope.

There are two ways you can photograph the stars. Each depends on how the camera is mounted. If it's placed on a tripod or some other solid mount, the stars will leave tracks as they slowly move across the sky.

Stars won't leave tracks if the camera is placed on a motor mount that is moving one degree to the ecliptic every four minutes. Instead, more stars will show up on film, stars that can't otherwise be seen. But motor mounts are expensive.

Both ways involve a simple photographic trick, one that you could never do in the daytime. Get a camera with a shutter that can be locked open. This leaves film exposed to all the light that comes through the shutter while it's open. When the camera is attached to a "solid" tripod on the earth, the stars seem to move. When the earth's movement is counteracted by the motor mount, the stars seem to stand still, and dimmer ones come out of hiding.

Sidereal Time

Sidereal time is star time, time kept by the stars. Astronomers tell sidereal time by picking any star and measuring how long it takes the star to return to the same spot in the sky one day, month, or year from now.

The earth's normal day — from one midnight to the next — is 24 hours. But the earth's sidereal day is 23 hours, 56 minutes, and 4 seconds, because the star rises 3 minutes and 56 seconds earlier than the sun every day. Earth's sidereal month is 27 days, 8 hours. The synodic month is 29 days, 12 hours.

Sidereal time works because stars are so far away. Actually the stars are moving. But over the vast distances of deep space, these movements seem very, very slight. They are measured only by astronomers using telescopes and other precise instruments. Compared with the sun, moon, and other objects in the solar system, the stars don't seem to move from their positions on the celestial sphere.

Synodic Time

Synodic time is earth time. It is time kept by the sun, instead of the stars. Synodic time is the time everyone normally goes by. A synodic day is 24 hours. A synodic month is 29½ days. A synodic year is 365¼ days.

Synodic time is slower than star time (sidereal) because the sun is closer to the earth than the stars are. This means the earth must rotate a little more before the sun or moon shows up in the same spot in the sky again.

Another use of synodic time is to tell how long a planet takes to orbit the sun, as that planet's orbit looks from earth. Distant planets like Neptune and Pluto

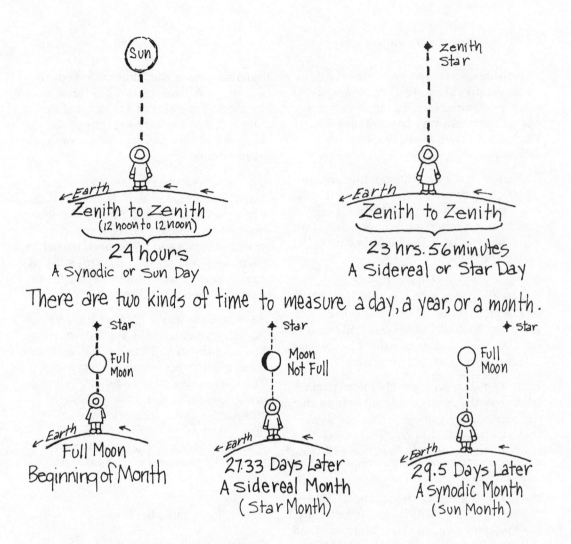

Sun

Earth
Zenith to zenith
(12 noon to 12 noon)
24 hours
A Synodic or Sun Day

zenith
star

Earth
Zenith to zenith
23 hrs. 56 minutes
A Sidereal or Star Day

There are two kinds of time to measure a day, a year, or a month.

star

Full Moon

Earth
Full Moon
Beginning of Month

star

Moon Not Full

Earth
27.33 Days Later
A sidereal Month
(Star Month)

star

Full Moon

Earth
29.5 Days Later
A synodic Month
(Sun Month)

need over a hundred years to complete one orbit around the sun — in sidereal time. But as seen from earth, these planets need a little over a year to complete one orbit. This is their synodic period.

A sidereal day is 4 minutes or 1 degree shorter than a synodic day. A sidereal month is 27.33 days. A synodic month is 29.5 days.

Almanacs and Ephemerides

A farmer's almanac will help you find the rising and setting times of the visible planets during the year. Most almanacs also contain information about the moon's phases and the times of sunrise and sunset.

An ephemeris will give more information than an almanac, including the object's exact location in the sky. The ephemeris is written for navigators, amateur astronomers, astrologers, and other serious skywatchers.

It takes a while to learn how to use either one of these yearly books. Any good almanac or ephemeris will have a clear explanation of how to use the timetables inside it. Don't let all the numbers scare you. These books are like a baseball box score in a newspaper. Once you understand them, they are easy to read.

Wandering the Planets

The word *planet* comes from an old Greek word, *planasthai*, which means "to spread out" or "to wander." This gives a clue as to how the ancients saw the planets. They knew that planets were special because they wander around the sky from night to night, while stars seem to stay in the same places.

People have yet to travel to another planet. Only 12 earthlings — all American astronauts — have wandered around on another sphere — the moon. Every other space traveler has cruised around earth or the moon in orbiting spaceships.

Instead of sending people, scientists have chosen to send machines to study the planets up close. Most of what is known about Mercury, Venus, Mars, and Jupiter has come from TV, radar, and measurements made on sophisticated spacecraft: Mariner, Pioneer, Viking.

If everything goes according to plan, American scientists will send two unmanned spacecraft on a "grand tour" of the outer planets in the late 1980s. This is a great time to go because the planets line up close to each other. The gravity of each planet will bend the courses of the spacecraft and reduce flight times. Instead of lasting decades, the trips will take no longer than nine years. But you don't have to wait that long to visit the planets. You can go on a tour of the solar system right now.

Planet Measurements

Each planet in this section has a box score with these items. Here's what each item means:

Average distance from sun is how far the planet is orbiting from the sun most of the time. During each planet's year, the sphere will move slightly closer and then slightly farther from the sun.

Diameter is the length of any line that passes through the center of a sphere, from one edge to the other.

Length of day is how long the planet takes to rotate once on its axis. Told in sidereal time, the day is based on the rising of a star, not the rising of the sun.

Length of year is how long it takes to complete one orbit. A sidereal year is one full orbit as seen from the planet. A synodic year is how long the planet takes to make one full orbit as it looks from the earth.

Tilt of orbit to ecliptic is how many degrees the planet's poles are tilted toward the very middle of the zodiac.

Greatest magnitude is the brightest the planet ever gets in the night sky.

Moons is how many natural satellites the planet has, if any.

Color is the color that sets one planet apart from others, not its brightness.

Mercury

With its face full of craters and cracks, Mercury looks like the moon in a mirror. Both the moon and Mercury are dry with almost no atmosphere. Both have a hot side and a cold side. Nothing we know would grow there.

This is not the moon! This is Mercury, the planet closest to the sun. The lines are caused by a photo-graphic process that fits several Mariner 10 pictures together into one clear picture of the planet. (NASA photo)

Ten years ago the face of Mercury was nothing more than a blob at the end of a telescope. Closest planet to the sun, Mercury hid from close observation. That was until 1974 when the Mariner 10 satellite "flew by" the planet. The satellite's TV cameras told a story that no telescope could, because they could see details on the surface down to the size of a football field.

The cameras showed that Mercury has its own personality, apart from the moon. It has hills and trenches unlike anything seen on the moon or Mars. Up to 80 percent of Mercury is iron, so it's the densest planet. The moon seems to be a balloon by comparison.

Mercury is three times closer to the sun than earth is. This planet also has a strange quirk in its orbit, which makes the sun seem to dance around in the same spot of Mercury's sky for about a week. Right under the sun is Mercury's "hot pole," a place where temperatures can reach 800 degrees F, eight times hotter than any summer noon on earth.

Where to Look for Mercury

Because it orbits nearest the sun, Mercury is the hardest planet to see. It doesn't really come out at night. It can only be seen in the morning or evening, never more than two hours after sunset or two hours before sunrise. The best times to see Mercury are after spring sunsets and before fall sunrises.

Mercury Measurements

average distance from sun: 36,000,000 miles

diameter: 3,010 miles

length of day: 58.65 earth days

length of year: 88 earth days (sidereal) 116 earth days (synodic)

tilt of orbit to ecliptic: 7 degrees

greatest magnitude: -1.9

color: lead gray

This isn't earth! This is Venus, the second planet from the sun. Venus is the planet that seems most like ours, no matter if it's seen from earth or from the Mariner 10 satellite, as in this picture. (NASA photo)

Venus

Venus is the planet that looks and seems the most like earth. It passes closer to earth than any other planet. It's about the same size as earth, and it too has swirling storms of white clouds. Yet Venus is one of the most mysterious objects in the night sky.

Earthlings have always been drawn to mysteries about Venus. One astronomer, Immanuel Velikovsky, argues that Venus was once a comet. The comet was "captured" by the sun and locked into its present orbit. Venus is the only planet that rotates clockwise, and Velikovsky says that this shows Venus was not one of the original planets. Many scientists call Velikovsky a quack and a crank.

With its swirling earthlike clouds, Venus looks very inviting, until you get right down to measuring and studying it. Mariner 10 did that in 1974 when it flew by the planet. Mariner instruments showed that Venus's clouds are deadly. The atmosphere is dense with carbon dioxide and sulfuric acid droplets, poisonous to humans. Even if you could breathe the air of Venus, you would not be able to stand up. Winds race at speeds sometimes faster than 200 mph, and the surface is 900 degrees F. Venus may be lovely to look at, but it's too hot to hold.

Where to Look for Venus

After the moon, the bright silvery light of Venus is the most spectacular sight in the night sky. Venus is always a morning or evening "star." It never shows up more than three hours before or after the sun.

Like the moon, Venus also goes through phases. The changing crescent of Venus can be seen with a seven-power telescope or with binoculars. Venus seems to move so much that it's best to use an almanac to find when it rises and sets.

Venus Measurements

average distance from sun: 67,200,000 miles

diameter: 7,620 miles

length of day: 243 earth days

length of year: 224.7 earth days (sidereal) 584 earth days (synodic)

tilt of orbit to ecliptic: 3 degrees 24 seconds

greatest magnitude: -4.4

color: bright silver

This is how earth looks without colors. You'll never see it this size, unless you travel to the moon someday! (NASA photo)

Earth

Earth is home. The Blue Planet. Full of water, sky, and life. Photographed from near space, it looks inviting. In the last two decades, astronauts and scientists have been rewriting the planetary history of earth. Instead of being a calm, kind place, earth seems to have gone through very violent periods, especially in the times long before life arose.

Geologists now believe that 200,000,000 years ago all land on earth was joined into one giant continent, which they call *Pangaea*. Oddly enough, Pangaea looked a lot like the early European maps of the world, although those maps were done long after the seven continents moved to their present positions. That's right! Geologists say the continents — Africa, North America, Europe, all of them — have moved across the face of the earth, on big "plates" of solid rock. Some of them are still moving. This idea has revised the earth sciences, such as geology and geography.

Based on satellite studies of Venus, astronomers believe that the earth would have been totally different if it had been a little closer to the sun and about ten degrees hotter when its early atmosphere was forming. Under those conditions all earth's water would have boiled off into space. Earth would be more like Venus, very hot and windy, with poisons in the air.

Earth Measurements

average distance from sun: 92,956,524.4 miles

diameter: 7,926.4 miles

length of day: 24 hours (synodic) 23 hours 56 minutes (sidereal)

length of year: 365.26 days

tilt of axis: 23 degrees 27 seconds

moons: one

Astronaut Charles M. Duke digs for moon samples at the edge of Plum Crater. Duke was a member of the Apollo 16 crew. And he was one of the first to ride a "car" on another sphere. See it on the other side of the crater? (NASA photo)

Earth's Moon

Scientists are still plowing through the blizzard of information that has piled up since the last Apollo moon walk in December, 1972. Six Apollo ships carried and returned with 12 astronauts who set up instruments and carried rocks from the moon's hot and dry surface. A total of 841 pounds of moon rocks and soil were brought back to earth. These are still being studied for clues to the mysteries of the solar system, as well as to the moon.

Apollo cleared up one moon mystery. That is, what happened to create the moon's largest "sea," the Mare Imbrium or Sea of Rains? This dry, flat moon basin is almost twice as wide as Texas. Most of the moon is hilly and bumpy. Why is this one spot so big and so level?

Scientists combing through the moon rocks believe that they now know the answer. Around 4,000,000,000 years ago, an asteroid or something big slammed into the moon. It hit with the force of a billion H-bombs. The moon's surface cracked and heaved for a thousand miles in every direction. The moon almost split in half, but instead, the cracks filled with lava. And the lava flowed out into the big impact crater to form the "sea." Slowly it cooled and cemented the moon's face. Today we see the Mare Imbrium as the right eye of the Man in the Moon.

Imbrium is a major landmark on the face and in the history of the earth's only natural satellite. Look at it on the next full moon. It's the big dark area on top (north) and a bit to the left of center.

Do you know the bright ray-crater Tycho on the south side of the moon? It's one of the brightest areas on the sphere, and it can be found easily on a rising full moon. It's the small crater at the bottom with all the long lines running off in all directions. Find a ray that leads straight north and slightly west. It will point to the Imbrium, right above Tycho in the moon's northern hemisphere.

Moon Measurements

diameter: 2,160 miles

length of month: 29 days, 12 hours, 44 minutes (synodic) 27 days, 7 hours, 43 minutes (sidereal)

tilt of orbit to ecliptic: 5 degrees 6 seconds

This is the north pole of Mars, photographed a special way to show the ridges and mountains, but **not** the bright polar cap covering of water ice. (NASA photo)

Mars

Astronomers have learned more about Mars in the last decade than any other planet. The sophisticated Viking — probably the most elaborate machine ever made — has flown around the Red Planet, mapped it, landed, dug into the soil, and tested it many times to look for life. Tests are still going on to tell if microbes or some other kind of soil life could survive on the cold and dusty surface. Some scientists believe Mars may now be like Earth was 200,000,000 years ago, an Ice Age planet. Even in summer, noontime temperatures on Mars are below 0 degrees.

Mars has sights unlike any seen elsewhere. The Valles Marineris, the grand canyon of Mars, is four miles deep and 3,000 miles long — long enough to cover the whole length of the United States. That's 100 times larger than earth's Grand Canyon, which would be just a scratch in the Valles Marineris. Mars also has the largest known volcanic mountain, Olympus Mons. It's 15 miles high — about three times higher than earth's Mount Everest rises above sea level.

Two moons, Deimos and Phobos, orbit Mars. Neither moon is sphere-shaped. Both of them look like deflated footballs.

Where to Look for Mars

The light from Mars is red and unblinking, so you can tell it from the stars, including the red giants which blink and twinkle. The trouble with Mars is that it is difficult to predict where it will be. Get an almanac or ephemeris to find when it can be seen.

The best time to view Mars is at opposition, when earth is between the sun and Mars. Then the planet rises at sunset and stays out all night. This happens once every 25 months. Mars will be at opposition in January 1978, February 1980, March 1982, and April 1984. These are also times of retrograde motion for Mars, when the planet seems to slip backwards (westward) in its orbit. You'll see more of Mars then. But to see surface markings, you'll need a telescope that magnifies things at least 200 times.

Mars Measurements

average distance from sun: 142,000,000 miles

diameter: 4,220 miles

length of day: 24 hours, 37 minutes

length of year: 687 earth days (sidereal) 780 earth days (synodic)

tilt of orbit to ecliptic: 1 degree 51 seconds

greatest magnitude: -2.8

moons: two

color: red

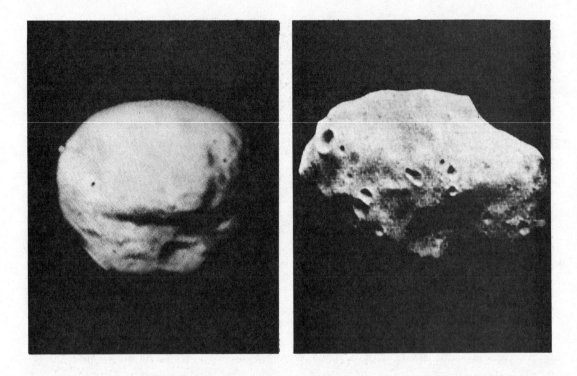

Deimos (left) and Phobos (right) are moons of Mars. They are not ball-shaped, like the earth's moon. Astronomers believe Phobos and Deimos may be asteroids that were "captured" by Mars's gravity. (NASA photo)

Asteroids

An asteroid with no name passed within 750,000 miles of earth in October, 1976. That's very close, although it was three times farther away than the moon. In 1937 an asteroid named Hermes came within 500,000 miles of earth.

What are asteroids? They are also called minor planets or planetoids. The words mean the same thing. Asteroids are floating rocks in space. They look more like cigars than spheres. Some are as big as mountains. Others are so small they

can't be measured. About 2,000 asteroids have been named and numbered.

Most asteroids twist and tumble in a broad path between Mars and Jupiter, but some have crazier orbits. They wander more through the solar system and come closer to earth.

Asteroids are one of the solar system's best mysteries, but no one really knows how they got there. Are they simply the remains of a shattered planet? Or are they the makings of a new one?

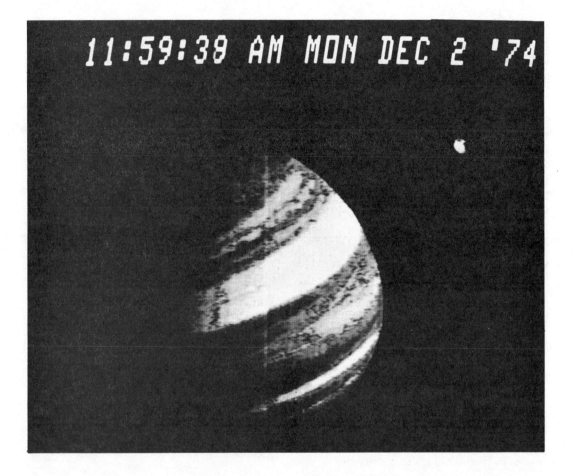

11:59:39 AM MON DEC 2 '74

Jupiter as seen by Pioneer 11's TV cameras. The bright dot is Ganymede, one of the planet's 12 moons. Some astronomers believe Ganymede has comfortable conditions for life! Maybe Jupiter and its moons are a "solar system" all by themselves. (NASA photo)

Jupiter

Jupiter is the biggest, fastest-moving planet, with many moons. It has no solid surface. None of that is what's really special about Jupiter, though. The planet doesn't really seem like a planet at all. It seems more like a star — a forming sun.

Jupiter gives off two-and-a-half times more heat than it gets from the sun. Although it is 11 times larger than the earth, Jupiter spins through one day in less than ten hours! The planet is still shrinking, and this is the big reason it spins so quickly. Except for one spot,

Jupiter's upper atmosphere runs in long bands around the planet. That one spot is the famous Red Spot. It seems to be a very old and gigantic storm, big enough for three earths to fit inside!

Jupiter has 12 moons. Four of them (Io, Europa, Callisto, and Ganymede) can be seen through binoculars, if the binoculars are held very steadily. Some astronomers believe Ganymede may be a place in the solar system to find life as we know it. On Ganymede, Jupiter would be warm and seem like the sun.

Two Pioneer spacecraft photographed the planet extensively in 1974. This is why astronomers know the distant sphere so well. These observations of Jupiter are causing some people to wonder if planets are nothing more than "stars" cooling off?

Where to Look for Jupiter

Jupiter, the second brightest planet, can be seen five months of the year in the morning sky. For five more months it moves in the evening sky before disappearing into daytime. Jupiter's orbit swings out of view behind the sun for two months each year. Then it reappears as a morning star. Use an almanac to find exactly when it rises and sets this year.

Jupiter takes about a year to move through one zodiac constellation. In the late 1970s, the planet will move through Gemini, Cancer, and Leo. In the early 1980s, Jupiter will travel across Leo, Virgo, Libra, and Scorpius.

Jupiter Measurements

average distance from sun: 484,000,000 miles

diameter: 88,800 miles

length of day: 9 hours, 52 minutes

length of year: 11.86 earth years (sidereal) 399 earth days (synodic)

tilt of orbit to ecliptic: 1 degree 18 seconds

greatest magnitude: -2.5

moons: 12

color: whitish yellow

Saturn

When Galileo first saw Saturn in his telescope, he thought he also saw "ears" on each side of the planet. Galileo had difficulty believing what he was seeing, because he didn't expect to find what was really there.

It took stronger telescopes to show that the "ears" of Saturn are really rings around the planet — rings of different colors. These bands extend out from the planet for 50,000 miles. Astronomers aren't sure how thin the rings are, maybe a few inches, maybe a few thousand feet. Astronomers also aren't sure what the rings are made of. Perhaps they are asteroidlike rocks coated with ice or maybe frozen snowballs.

Before 1980 a Mariner satellite is scheduled to "fly by" Saturn and clear up the mystery of the planet's rings. The satellite may also show us some of Saturn's 10 moons. We don't know much about them because telescopes can't pick up surface details.

Earth's view of Saturn's rings changes over the years at a regular cycle. The late 1970s and 1980s are good times to see the rings because they are tilted more toward earth at those times. Some people can see Saturn's rings through binoculars, but they must be held steady by a tripod or something.

Where to Look for Saturn

Saturn is the most distant planet you can see with unaided eyes. It's so far away that it takes 30 years to move around the zodiac. Once you find it, Saturn is easy to locate night after night, because it stays in one constellation for two-and-a-half years. During the end of the 1970s, Saturn will move from Leo to Virgo. In the first half of the 1980s, the ringed planet will show up in Libra and Scorpius.

For about two months each year, Saturn can't be seen as it passes behind the sun. But it reappears as a morning star and rises two hours earlier with each passing month. The planet remains about the same distance from earth, so it always seems the same size.

Saturn Measurements

average distance from sun: 886,000,000 miles

diameter: 74,000 miles

length of day: 10 hours, 26 minutes

length of year: 29.46 earth years (sidereal) 378 earth days (synodic)

tilt of orbit to ecliptic: 2 degrees 29 seconds

greatest magnitude: -.2

moons: 10

color: yellow

Uranus

The seventh planet, Uranus, wasn't known to the ancients, because they didn't have telescopes or binoculars. The closest it ever gets to earth is 1,610,000,000 miles. At that distance from earth, hundreds of stars seem brighter, so earthlings couldn't tell this planet from one of the stars.

Near the end of the American Revolution, British astronomer Sir William Herschel discovered Uranus while scanning the skies with one of the largest telescopes of the time. Herschel thought he had found a comet. Other astronomers continued to believe Uranus was a star. But later studies of the object's movement proved it couldn't be a comet or a star, because it orbits the sun.

No NASA satellites have traveled past Uranus, so many of its mysteries must wait until a Pioneer or Mariner photographs it. One of the mysteries that excites astronomers most is the spin of Uranus's axis.

The planet spins on its side, very rapidly. The rotation of Uranus is not even half as long as an earth day. Some days at the equator, the sun would seem to circle in the sky! And for 42 years, each pole of the planet would be locked on the dark side where it wouldn't get sunlight at all. The three outer planets, including Uranus, can't be seen with bare eyes.

Uranus Measurements

average distance from sun: 1,780,000,000 miles

diameter: 29,500 miles

length of day: 10 hours, 45 minutes

length of year: 84 earth years (sidereal) 369.7 earth days (synodic)

tilt of orbit to ecliptic: 46 seconds

greatest magnitude: 5.7

moons: 100?

Neptune

The existence of a new planet beyond Saturn caused a big headache for 18th century astronomers. The new planet, Uranus, orbits with a funny wobble. Astronomers knew something big must cause the wobble, but they didn't know what it was. Mathematicians helped tackle the problem. In 1846 they found a reason for the wobble. It was an eighth planet, orbiting outside Uranus and tugging on it, pulling it slightly when their orbits came close. The new planet was named Neptune, after the Roman god of the sea.

Before they realized it was a planet, astronomers had always considered Neptune just another speck in their telescopes. Now they know it is a planet, but not much else. It's too far away to see surface details clearly. Neptune will have to wait its turn to be photographed by a satellite, perhaps in the next few years, after Saturn and Uranus get their chance to pose close-up for the cameras.

Neptune Measurements

average distance from sun: 2,800,000,000 miles

diameter: 27,200 miles

length of day: 15 hours, 48 minutes

length of year: 164.8 earth years (sidereal) 367.5 earth days (synodic)

tilt of orbit to ecliptic: 1 degree 48 seconds

greatest magnitude: 7.6

moons: 2

Pluto

In the early 1900s astronomers were still perturbed by wobbles in the orbits of Uranus and Neptune. In fact these wobbles became known as "perturbations." Astronomers knew something big must be disturbing these orbits, probably a ninth planet. But where was it?

It took almost 30 years of tedious searching, but finally astronomer Clyde Tom-baugh picked Pluto out of a photograph containing more than a million stars.

Pluto is a real wanderer. Some astronomers believe that the ninth planet is an "escaped satellite" of Neptune. At one time Pluto was the third and farthest moon from Neptune. But Triton, the second moon of Neptune, moved very close to Pluto. No one is exactly sure how it happened, but Pluto picked up enormous speed, enough to escape the gravity of Neptune, and dash into its new orbit. This may help explain why Pluto's orbit is tilted so much to the ecliptic and why the planet spends part of its orbit passing inside Neptune's path.

Pluto is certainly a cold and dark place. The sun would seem to be just another star in its sky. But until satellites photograph it, Pluto will remain only a dim dot in the biggest telescopes.

Pluto Measurements

average distance from sun: 3,660,000,000 miles

diameter: 3,600 miles

length of day: 6.39 earth days

length of year: 247.7 earth years (sidereal) 366.7 earth days (synodic)

tilt of orbit to ecliptic: 17 degrees

greatest magnitude: 14.5

moons: probably none

Pluto is so dim that it's even hard to see under the arrow in this picture. The bright star to the left is Wasat, located in Gemini. It's the only object in this photo that can be seen without a telescope. (Lowell Observatory photo)

Undiscovered Planets

Nobody can be certain that our solar system has only nine planets and no more. But nobody can be sure there are others waiting to be discovered, either.

Certainly, any undiscovered planets would be small and dim, otherwise, astronomers would have found them. Of course, the smaller a planet is, the harder it is to find. But astronomers are always looking for clues that might point to another wanderer around the sun.

FIND THAT CONSTELLATION: ELEVEN

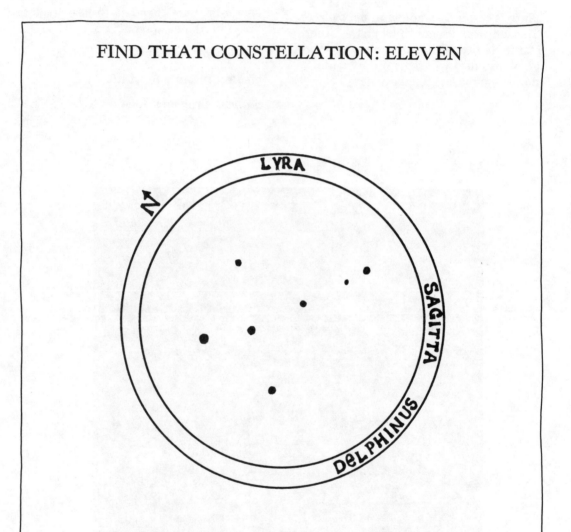

This whole constellation fits right inside the Milky Way. This is also the home of the "Dumbbell Nebula."

Hint: Some people think it's a cross. Others believe it's a bird.

When to look for it: Rises in summer and is at its high point in September. If you live far enough north, it will never set. Otherwise it goes down after November.

Answer on page 102.

Cycle Around the Solar System

Do you know how big the solar system is? It's not hard to find out. All you need to do is to have one small scavenger hunt. And go on one long bicycle ride.

First the scavenger hunt. Look around and try to round up the ten items in this list. None of them is hard to find. And you can substitute any one with another item, as long as it's round and about the same size. Here's the list:

Put all the items in a bag or basket. Stick a bookmark in this page so you can take the book along. Hop on your bicycle and head for the nearest empty, school football field. You, your bike, your book, and your bag of goodies are going to take a little trip around the solar system, to find out how big it really is. See you at the track.

A football field (100 yards) and an oval track (440 yards) are two standard units

A Solar System Salad

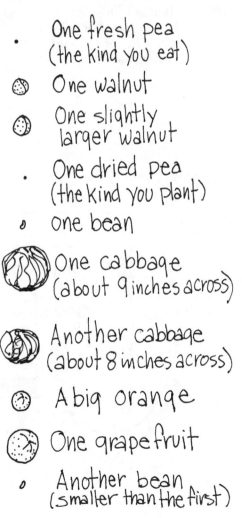

- One fresh pea (the kind you eat)
- One walnut
- One slightly larger walnut
- One dried pea (the kind you plant)
- one bean
- One cabbage (about 9 inches across)
- Another cabbage (about 8 inches across)
- A big orange
- One grapefruit
- Another bean (smaller than the first)

99

of measure found almost anywhere in the United States. But instead of going around a football field on a boring old track, imagine that you are speeding through the solar system.

At this scale, each yard you travel is equal to 211,265 real miles in space. Bet you've never ridden a bicycle that fast before! If you start on the track at the football goal line, you'll be past the sun by the five-yard line.

You'll briefly stop at each planet as you reach it. At each stop, drop off the planet from your bag of goodies. Mercury's pea, Venus's walnut . . . and so on. Notice that after the first lap-and-a-half, you've gone through half of the solar system — the terrestrial planets, or the hard ones with a surface you could walk on.

The Terrestrial Lap

Mercury is a fresh pea at 36,000,000 miles or 2/5 lap.

Venus is a walnut at 67,200,000 miles or 3/4 lap.

Earth is a bigger walnut at 92,956,524.4 miles or one lap.

The *Moon* is a dried pea, one step away.

Mars is a bean at 142,000,000 miles or 1½ laps.

Rest briefly after Mars, but not too long, because you've only started your journey! Next are the Jovian planets — mostly big and very far away. After you reach Saturn, stop and eat the peas, walnuts, and cabbages. You'll need all the energy you can muster to get to Pluto.

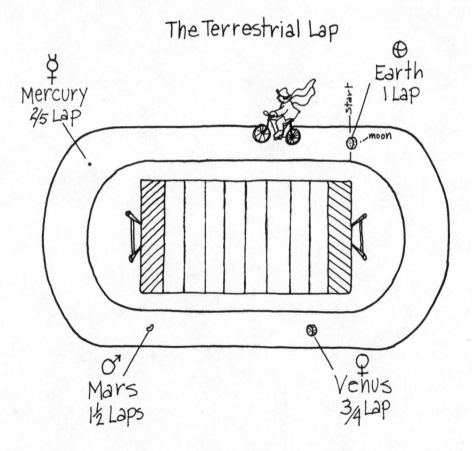

The Terrestrial Lap

☿
Mercury
2/5 Lap

⊕
Earth
1 Lap

Start

..moon

♂
Mars
1½ Laps

♀
Venus
3/4 Lap

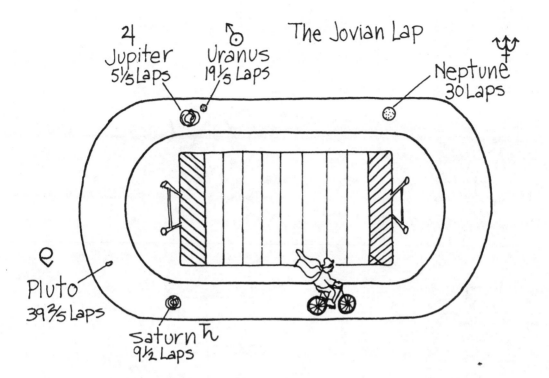

The Jovian Lap

Jupiter is a nine-inch cabbage at 484,000,000 miles or 5 1/5 laps.

Saturn is an eight-inch cabbage at 886,000,000 miles or 9 1/2 laps.

Uranus is an orange at 1,780,000,000 miles or 19 1/5 laps.

Neptune is a grapefruit at 2,800,000,000 miles or 30 laps.

Pluto is a bean at 3,660,000,000 miles or 39 2/5 laps.

Why does it take less than two laps to go through the first half of the solar system and almost 38 more laps to reach the last known planet? Do you see why it took so long for earthlings to discover Uranus, Neptune, and Pluto?

The Astronomical Unit

Light years are too long to be useful in measuring the distances between planets, moons, and other objects in the solar system. Astronomers have chosen a more convenient unit of measurement for this purpose — the astronomical unit.

The length of one astronomical unit is the average distance between earth and sun. This distance is about 92,956,600 miles, but that doesn't matter exactly. The important thing is the ratio, or relative distances, between planets.

Using astronomical units the relative distances between the planets always stay the same, no matter if the distances are told in inches, centimeters, football

fields, or actual miles. Here are the relative distances between the planets. They are told in astronomical units:

Mercury	.39
Venus	.72
Earth	1.00
Mars	1.52
Asteroids	2.33
Jupiter	5.20
Saturn	9.52
Uranus	19.16
Neptune	29.99
Pluto	39.37

Answer to Find That Constellation Eleven: Cygnus (see map, page 122)

Solar System Models

Do you have trouble remembering which planet is closest to the sun or fifth from the sun? If you make a model of the solar system, it will remind you how the planets line up.

There are many ways to make the model. And it can always be proportional — the way the planets are really placed in space — if you use the astronomical unit. Pick some unit of length that you're familiar with such as an inch, a football field, a mile, the distance from your home to a friend's.

Let that distance be equal to one astronomical unit. Mark off that length on a piece of paper or something. Put the sun at one end of the line and the earth at the other. From there it's easy to figure out the spacings of the other planets by using astronomical units.

For example, if you picked one inch as your model astronomical unit, all the planets would be spaced like this:

Mercury	2/5 inch
Venus	3/4 inch
Earth	1 inch
Mars	1 1/2 inches
Asteroids	2 1/3 inches
Jupiter	5 1/5 inches
Saturn	9 1/2 inches
Uranus	19 1/5 inches
Neptune	30 inches
Pluto	39 2/5 inches

Pinhead Solar System

Here's one easy way to make a scale-sized solar system. Get a package of glassheaded pins, the kind people use for sewing. Pick the pack with the most variety of colors. If you look closely, you'll see that each pinhead is slightly different.

Pick one pin for each planet. Make your choices based on the color, shape, and "personality" of the planet. Let the bigger ones be Jupiter and Saturn and the smaller ones be Pluto, Mercury, and Mars.

If you choose one inch for your astronomical unit, you can make a solar system that will easily fit into your room. If you pick larger units, a foot or a yard or a meter, you'll have to go outside to fit in Pluto and the other distant planets.

5

Star and Light

Night Lights
and Shooting Stars

The earth's atmosphere is a very creative force. It creates many of the odd stars, weird lights, bright flashes, glows, and UFOs that lots of people think come from outer space. The zodiacal light, counterglow, auroras, meteor showers, and rings around the moon can all be seen by observant eyes without optical aids. Most of these sky events happen regularly, so you can learn when to watch for them.

Shooting stars aren't stars at all, they're meteors. Meteors are mostly small chunks of nickel and iron or broken bits of a comet. They fly through the sky and burn up. Usually.

Once in a very long while, a meteor will reach the earth's surface. Meteor Crater, a big hole in the Arizona Desert, is the mark made by a meteor many thousands of years ago. Meteors make streaks in

Meteors

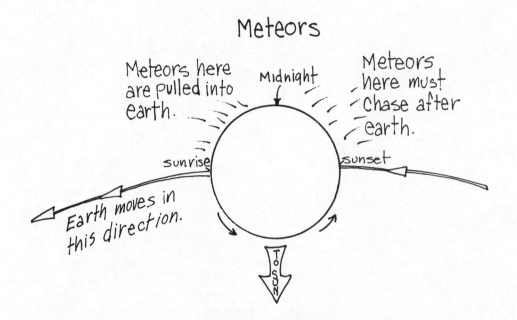

Meteors here are pulled into earth.

Midnight

Meteors here must chase after earth.

sunrise

sunset

Earth moves in this direction.

TO SUN

the sky. Big meteors are called fireballs. Meteors that hit the earth are called meteorites. Fortunately, most meteorites are small.

Most meteors are seen after midnight and before sunrise. Do you know why? The diagram above will help you figure this out.

Watching for Meteors

After you know when to look for them, you'll have to wait for them. Watching

for meteors takes patience. They are best seen on a clear moonless night, or after the moon has gone down. But on some nights of the year, you can't miss them. Some meteors happen in showers. It's easy to spot them because they show up in the same constellations around the same time each year.

Auroras

If you don't like to visit cold places, you won't see many auroras. Auroras

Meteor shower	Dates	Constellation
Quadrantids	January 1-4	Bootes
Lyrids	April 20-22	Lyra
Eta Aquarids	May 1-11	Aquarius
Delta Aquarids	July 24-August 16	Aquarius
Perseids	July 27-August 17	Perseus
Orionids	October 15-25	Orion
Taurids	October 26-November 16	Taurus
Leonids	November 15-17	Leo
Geminids	December 9-14	Gemini

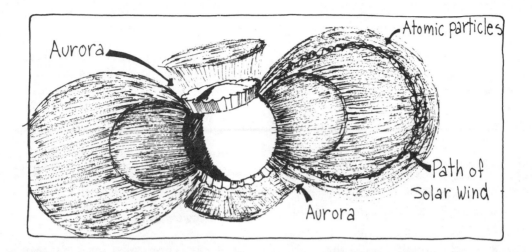

Aurora

Atomic particles

Aurora

Path of Solar Wind

are sky lights that happen around both poles of the earth. Most people know them by their common names, the northern lights (aurora borealis) and the southern lights (aurora australis).

Auroras look a lot like curtains in the sky. They are long wavy bands of light caused by the earth's magnetic field. The sun is always sending out pieces of excited atoms in all directions. This is known as the solar wind. When these excited atomic particles reach earth's magnetic field they speed up and collide with molecules in the atmosphere high above the North and South Poles. This creates the long bands of light.

Watching for Auroras

The best place to see the aurora borealis is northern Alaska and Canada. There people see them two out of three clear nights. As you move south the chances of seeing auroras decrease.

Zodiacal Light

Finding this wedge-shaped blur is a good test of anyone's ability as a night sky observer. The zodiacal light is very dim, but some people can see it when their eyes are adjusted to the dark.

The best times to look are February and March after sunset or before dawn in September and October. It is seen only 90 minutes after sunset on the western horizon — or 90 minutes before sunrise in the east.

The glow has a definite wedge shape. It slants into the direction of the zodiac. Find the zodiac by marking the point on the horizon where the sun sets.

Counterglow

The glow of the zodiacal light has a partner, the counterglow. This is even more difficult to see. Give yourself 30 minutes in the dark to let your eyes adapt before you start looking for it.

Counterglow only happens at true midnight. True midnight is at a full 180 degrees from noon. In summer look for it at 11 p.m., if your town is on daylight-saving time.

The glow has no regular shape. It is very dim but should be at the point directly opposite the sun. It's hard to see it any other time besides new moon.

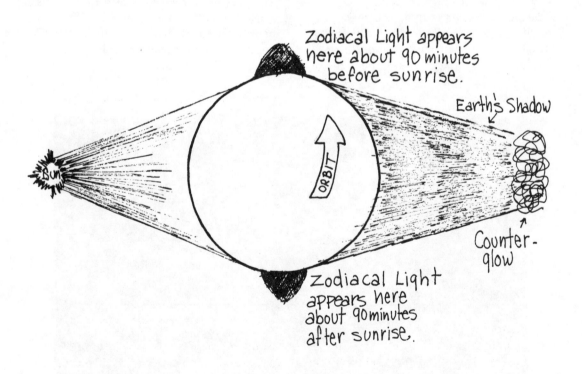

Zodiacal Light and Counterglow

Zodiacal Light appears here about 90 minutes before sunrise.

Earth's Shadow

ORBIT

Counter-glow

Zodiacal Light appears here about 90 minutes after sunrise.

FIND THAT CONSTELLATION: TWELVE

The fifth brightest northern star is found in this constellation. Once it contained a star that grew to become the second largest star in the sky. Now that star is barely visible through telescopes.

Hint: This bird may not love America, but America loves this bird.

When to look for it: Rising in June, it reaches the zenith in September. By November it begins to set.

Answer on page 112.

How Far Is a Star?

Stars seem far away, and their distances are measured by a speedometer that makes a million miles seem microscopic. But actually the stuff of stars isn't far away at all. It's right here. Below your feet. Inside you. All around you.

You Are a Star

No one knows all there is to know about atoms. Actually it's very difficult to picture something that small and that fast. And no one has a microscope powerful

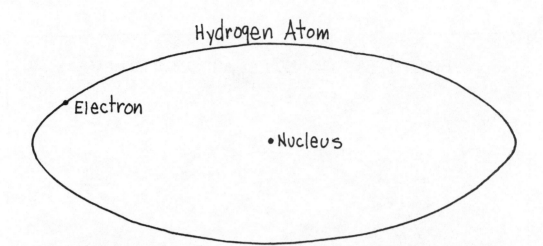

Hydrogen Atom

•Electron

•Nucleus

enough to see one. In the mind, one atom gets as lost as one star does hiding in the universe.

People are made of the same atoms that stars are. The atoms are just arranged differently. People and stars have vastly different masses, different sizes, and different purposes. But they are all made of the same basic atoms.

Comets, meteors, dust clouds, and supernovas spread the stuff of space around the universe. The same atoms that create the people, earth, sun, and the rest of the solar system can also be found in other galaxies. Space might look empty, but it is all connected.

One hydrogen atom does not actually look like the drawing above. The electron is too close to the nucleus here. An atom is mostly empty space.

The Life of a Star

Just like any other form of life, a star is born. As it grows and ages, it becomes an individual. It develops a "starality" like persons have personalities. After going through its different stages, the star dies.

All stars do not go through the same stages. It depends on what kind of atoms are in the star, how many of them there are, and how they are held together.

Astronomers try to tell the story of a star from a spectrum analysis of the star. They split the star's light to study its colors. These colors and the way they fit together tell astronomers something about what the star is made of and where it is going.

Twin Stars

Some astronomers believe that half the stars in the universe may be binaries. Binaries are twin stars. They're not like the sun because they do not shine alone. Instead, two (or more) stars revolve around one spot in space.

Astronomers can tell that stars are twins by using careful and exact measurement methods. Sometimes one star will cause the other to slowly "blink," as in Perseus with the bright twin star Algol. Other times two stars will cause slight changes in each other's position in the sky. Sirius has a nearby companion star that causes it to wobble. These wobbles and blinks show up in telescopes and spectroscopes, where astronomers measure and catalog them.

Answer to Find That Constellation Twelve: Aquila (see map, page 122)

The Pleiades are also known as the Seven Sisters. Squint your eyes and look at the picture. How many Sisters do you see? Actually more than 3,000 stars are floating in this young star system. Find the Pleiades on Maps One and Three on pages 28 and 70. (Yerkes Observatory Photo)

Sometimes stars look like twins or are called twins, but they're not. Castor and Pollux, in the constellation Gemini, are called the Twins, but they aren't binaries because they are many light years apart.

Blinking and Winking Stars

All stars twinkle because their light has to pass through earth's dense atmosphere. But stars also wink and blink. This is not caused by anything on earth. It's caused by the atomic nature of the stars themselves. These kinds of stars are called "variables." This means the light varies or changes during a certain period of time.

Astronomers have studied variable stars in several constellations, including Gemini, Taurus, Lyra, Cygnus, Cepheus. The Delta Cepheid variable has a very regular pulse rate that changes over a 10.2-day period. Astronomers know how to predict the pulse of this star so well that it has become the "standard candle" for measuring distances in deep space.

Nova and Supernova

Small stars, like the sun, lead quiet lives. Big stars with lots of mass are another story. A star 16 times more massive than the sun will only live 1/1,000 as long. When they die, these big stars do not go out quietly.

Many "go nova." They suddenly become very big and bright. Rare ones become supernovas so bright that they can be seen in the daytime! Supernovas blow off large amounts of matter, and this spreads through nearby space. Without supernovas, the complex elements that make up life would not be scattered so widely throughout the universe.

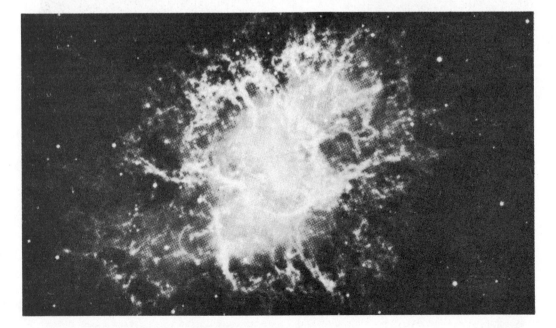

More astronomers study this splotch than any other object outside the solar system. The Crab Nebula, an expanding cloud of gas, may not look much like a crab now, but it's all that remains of a supernova seen all around the earth in 1054 A.D. At the center of the "Crab" is a very interesting pulsing star that is best seen through radio telescopes. The Crab Nebula is located in Taurus, see Map Three. (Lick Observatory Photo)

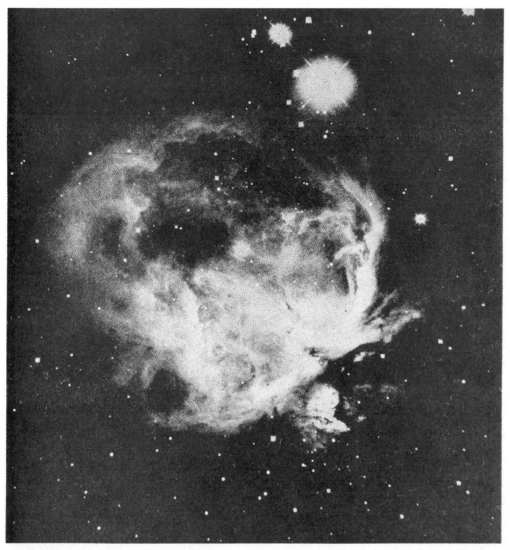

Look at Orion if you get a chance to gaze through a good telescope in winter. You'll see that the middle star in the Hunter's sword isn't a star at all. It's the great gas nebula, the cloudy object in the middle of this photo. Otherwise with unaided eyes this nebula looks like any other faint star. See Map Three to locate the Orion Nebula. (Yerkes Observatory photo)

Nebulae

Nebulae are clouds of gas, dust, and stuff in space. Astronomers recognize two kinds of nebulae — planetary and diffuse.

Planetary nebulae are not really planets as was first believed. Each is the remains of a star that went nova. The rest of the star can be found inside the planetary nebula.

Diffuse nebulae may be the beginnings of new stars. They look like faint veils. Many diffuse nebulae are so faint that they cannot be seen by anything but film. It is possible to see one diffuse nebula with unaided eyes. Look for it under the belt of Orion.

Quasars, Pulsars, and Other Oddballs

One of the biggest problems of our time is how to best use the limited energy on the earth. However there are objects in space that make our energy problems seem ridiculous by comparison. It is difficult for astronomers to call these objects "stars." Their inner workings are baffling to modern scientists. During your lifetime, these will be one of the biggest riddles astronomers have to solve.

Quasars are the most energetic bodies in the known universe. The radio astronomers who first located them called them "Quasi-Stellar Objects." The energy blasting out of one quasar could match a thousand galaxies! In a year the quasar will hurl off more energy than the sun will in its lifetime. Quasars are very far away and you won't see one unless you have a radio telescope.

Pulsars are something else again. Pulsars are very intense and very fast objects that seem to be lighthouses in space. Astronomers call them "rotating neutron stars." They are very dense and very small, compared with other stellar objects. They have intense magnetic fields, and they spin very fast, up to 1,000 rev-

olutions per second. There is a pulsar in the Crab Nebula of Taurus. It flashes at 30 pulses per second.

Black Holes

One sort of star is so mysterious that there's no way to describe or picture what happens there. The problem is this: no light or anything else can escape from this kind of star. In fact, it's not quite right to call it a star.

Some astronomers call these unseen objects "black holes." They are almost the complete opposite of a star. A star shines and gives off light. But a black hole is like a big vacuum cleaner that pulls everything into it, including light. This isn't science fiction. But it isn't fact yet either. Some astronomers are using x-ray telescopes to search for black holes. But it's very hard to find something that is darker than deep space.

You'll never be able to see a black hole, but you can find the parts of the night sky where astronomers are looking for them. Three likely spots are in or near the Milky Way; one in Cygnus, the Swan; another in Hercules; and a strange and giant dark object in Auriga.

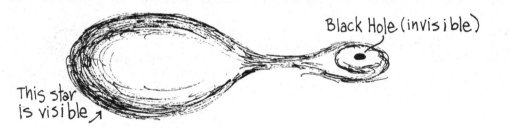

Black Hole (invisible)

This star is visible ↗

No one can see a black hole but astronomers believe it works like this. All of the material from the large star on the left is sucked into the small hole at the center of the disk on the right.

Galaxies and Galactic Clusters

Galaxies are groups of stars. Galactic clusters are groups of galaxies. If you could map the whole universe, galaxies would be the cities. Galactic clusters would be the states. But if you did that, these clusters would be found closer together than cities seem to be grouped in the states.

Maybe. No one is exactly sure because no one is far enough away to see it all at once.

One of the great beauties and mysteries of the universe is that all things — atoms, planets, stars, galaxies, clusters — seem to clump together around some axis or other point of revolution. No matter where they are.

M13, the "globular cluster" in Hercules, seems to be a dense ball of yellow and white light. In fact, it's several million stars. This dense galaxy can be seen without a telescope. Use Map Four to find it. (Hale Observatories photo)

This is how the Milky Way would look if you could gaze back at it from 2,200,000 light years away. Our sun and planet would be lost somewhere on the hazy edge of the galaxy. Actually this is another galaxy, M31 or the Great Spiral in Andromeda. Find it on Map One. (Yerkes Observatory photo)

The Milky Way

Earthlings live in a galaxy commonly called the Milky Way. It gets that name because it looks like milk spilling all across the sky. Before the invention of electricity, people saw the Milky Way more often. To find it you need to look on a dark night, away from city lights.

From another galaxy, the Milky Way might look more like a whirlpool. But we only know the galaxy we're in by the way it looks edge on — from inside, looking out.

The Milky Way is a good and bad place for star gazing. There are several interesting nebulae, star clusters, and strange stars in or near the galaxy. But because there is so much light around it, it's hard to pick out small objects and stars in the Milky Way.

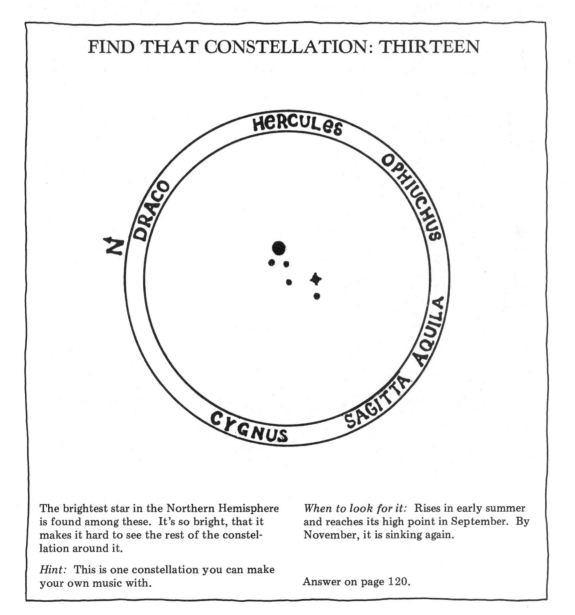

FIND THAT CONSTELLATION: THIRTEEN

The brightest star in the Northern Hemisphere is found among these. It's so bright, that it makes it hard to see the rest of the constellation around it.

Hint: This is one constellation you can make your own music with.

When to look for it: Rises in early summer and reaches its high point in September. By November, it is sinking again.

Answer on page 120.

119

How Long Is a Light Year?

Starlight is old stuff. Betelgeuse, the red giant star in Orion, is 500 light years away. In the same constellation, Rigel is a more distant cousin of 1,300 light years. This doesn't mean it would take 1,300 years for a starship to get to Rigel. It takes that long just for the star's *light* to get here.

The light you see any night from Polaris is 300 years old. Nobody had ever heard of the United States or the Oakland Raiders when the light left the star.

The sun is the nearest star. Sunlight takes eight minutes to reach earth. What if the sun went out five minutes ago? No one on earth would know it for another three minutes.

Answer to Find That Constellation Thirteen: Lyra (see map, page 122)

Five light years is the average distance between stars in a galaxy. Our galaxy, the Milky Way, is 100,000 light years wide. The average distance between galaxies is 1,000,000 light years. The farthest galaxies are seen as fuzzy blobs in the most powerful telescopes. These blobs are about 2,000,000,000 light years away. But no one is sure, because this is a very rough guess.

These distances are so phenomenal that no one from here could ever get there by any known way of travel. Some stars are so far away that it seems useless sometimes to even think about.

Figure a Light Year

Although it is based on the fastest thing we see, a light year is not a measure of speed. It is a measure of distance. Light years are used to measure the sizes of galaxies and the distances between stars. But how far is a light year? Get a pencil and look at the chart below. You figure it out. But if you don't own this book, get a pad and pencil and copy this chart first.

Miles	*Kilometers*
186,300 mi per second	300,000 km per second
x60	x60
.... per minute	.... per minute
x60	x60
....................per hour	.... per hour
x24	x24
.... per day	.... per day
x360	x360
.... per year	.... per year

FIND THAT CONSTELLATION: BONUS

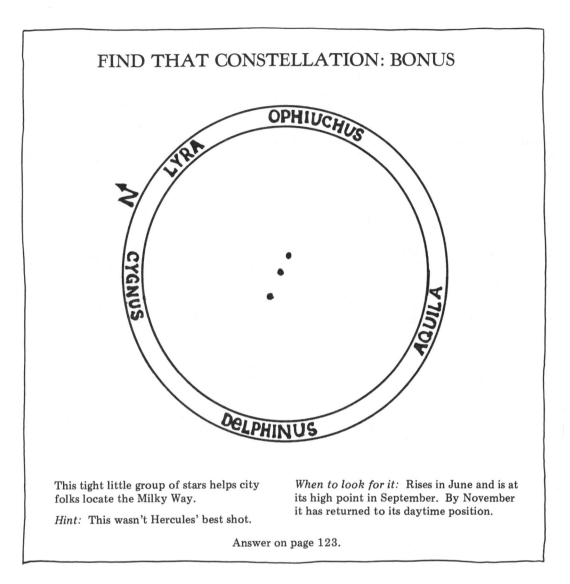

This tight little group of stars helps city folks locate the Milky Way.

Hint: This wasn't Hercules' best shot.

When to look for it: Rises in June and is at its high point in September. By November it has returned to its daytime position.

Answer on page 123.

FIND THOSE CONSTELLATIONS: MAP FOUR

Answers for Find That Constellation games Eleven, Twelve, Thirteen, and the Bonus Constellation are on the map, page 122. You can see these stars in the summer sky. They will be directly overhead at these times: late July (10 p.m.), late August (8 p.m.), late September (6 p.m.).

This is the midsummer night sky. It's full of music, giants, and birds. The birds are Cygnus (the Swan) and Aquila (the Eagle). The music comes from the Lyre, an old Greek string instrument that's a small version of a harp. The giants are Hercules and Ophiuchus.

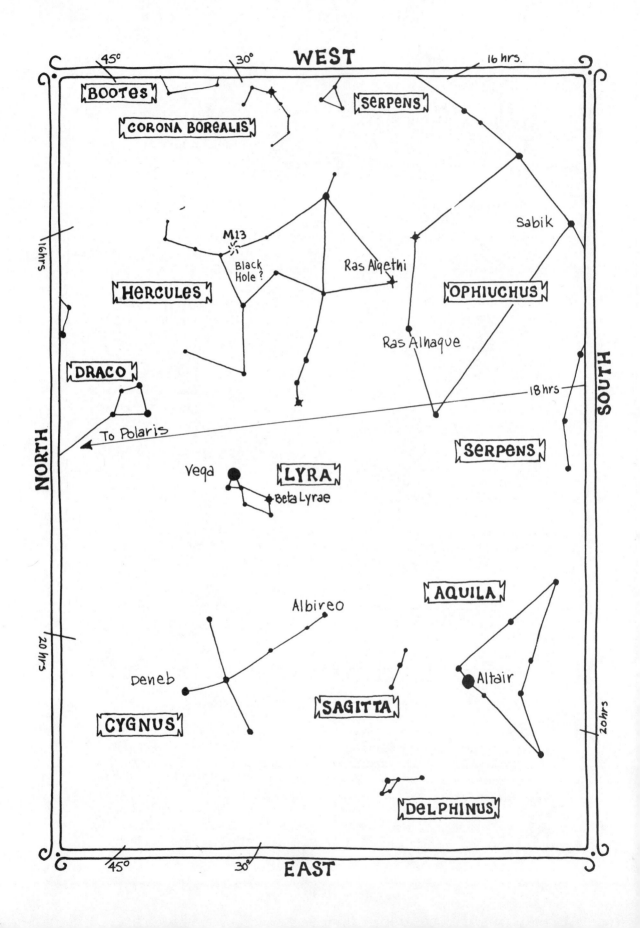

You've heard of Hercules, but what do you know of Ophiuchus? It's a gigantic constellation that tangles with Serpens and crosses the ecliptic. It could have been the 13th sign of the zodiac, but no one seemed willing to say "I'm an Ophiuchus."

Cygnus, the Swan, is also known as the Northern Cross. The whole constellation fits inside the Milky Way. The bright star, Deneb, marks the Swan's tail feathers. Albireo is at the Swan's head as it flies south. Albireo is not very bright, but it is a beautiful two-color double star. Cygnus is in good binocular area, because it's in the Milky Way. Clusters, clouds, and variable stars fill the field. The large "Dumbbell Nebula" is also located here. Cygnus is the location of another candidate for a black hole, Cygnus X-1. X-ray telescopes have measured strange things in this area.

Aquila, the Eagle, crosses the equator and points to Sagittarius, a zodiac constellation in the southern skies. Altair is the fifth brightest northern star. Part of Aquila is in the Milky Way. Lots of interesting objects which can be seen with telescopes or binoculars are hiding here for advanced amateur astronomers. Come back to this one when you get your telescope!

Lyra, the Harp, is a small but well-defined group. Vega is the brightest star in the northern night sky. Because it's so bright, Vega makes it harder to see other nearby stars in the constellation. What looks like one star, Beta Lyrae, might be two stars so close together that they're shaped like hard-boiled eggs. Epsilon Lyrae is a tight double star that really looks like a double to unaided eyes (not shown).

Answer to Find That Constellation Bonus: Sagitta, the Arrow (see map, opposite)

Other Pointers

Hercules is often pictured head to head with the other giant Ophiuchus. This giant is so large that it leads from Hercules to Scorpio and Sagittarius on the zodiac in the southern sky.

The Colors of Night

Nearly everyone has been fascinated by the colors of the western skies at sunset, but have you ever noticed how the colors of the eastern sky change as night falls? How about the northern and southern skies? Have you watched as the whole sky changes from bright light blue to darkest night?

The end of a bright cloudless day is the best time to see different blankets of color in the atmosphere. If you let your eyes adjust to darkness before you look, you can see different layers of air all across the sky. Each layer has a distinct color and brightness. The colors should look like this as the sun sets:

Blue / Pale Blue / White	one hour before sunset
Blue / Pale Blue / White / Pale Orange	20 minutes before sunset
Blue / White Yellow / Orange Purple Red / Dark Grey Blue	4 minutes before sunset
Red / Purple / Dark Grey Blue	12 minutes after sunset
Purple Red / Grey Blue / Soft Purple	20 minutes after sunset

Don't try to see all these colors in just one viewing. It will take many nights before you can spot all of them. But with practice you'll be able to see these bands more distinctly. It will be easier to see them in summer or autumn. Some experts say the best purples can be seen on the first clear evening after a string of spring rains.

Painters, musicians, jugglers, travelers, stargazers, and other lighthearted people try to see every sunset they can. Some of them have special techniques for taking the whole scene into view. Here's one.

Hold a small mirror out at arm's length. This way you can see other parts of the sky change as the sun goes down. Where does the sky get darkest first?

Every instant of every hour, night is falling somewhere on earth. As the sun goes down where you are tonight, stare at the first star you see rising on the eastern horizon. Do you know the star's name? Do you know the constellation it's in? Are you sure it's a star and not a planet, satellite, or something else?

What if the star were an eye that could stare at you? What would you do? Would you wink at it and hope it winks back? Would you ask it a question? Or would you just want it to stop staring at you?

Day passes completely into night and more stars join the bright one you first saw at sunset. You'll know the names of some of these. Others won't have names. As you learn more stars and constellations, you'll begin to feel more comfortable under the friendly blanket of the night sky. You'll know names and faces in the stars as they change through the seasons. You'll be familiar with them when they return next year.

Tonight everyone will sleep, including you. Sleep well under the sky's blanket. May the stars watch over you and wish well upon you.